Words From War

Written by **WE:ARE**

Compiled by **Miss Yankey**

Words From Warrior Women

Written by WE:ARE

Compiled by Miss Yankey

This book is dedicated to the women whose stories were never told, to the silenced and forgotten. Our hearts are with the women who didn't make it, who are still fighting, and who are free but healing. Always.

Table of Contents

WE : ARE
STRONGER TOGETHER

FOREWORD

In the face of adversity, the strength that resides within us often remains hidden, buried deep beneath layers of pain and fear. Yet, when women gather, empowering one another with shared experiences and boundless empathy, those hidden strengths become illuminated. Such is the profound journey chronicled within the pages of this heartfelt collection, *Words From Warrior Women*.

This anthology is not merely a compilation of poems; it is an inspiring testament to the resilience and courage of survivors of domestic violence who stepped forward to heal, empower, and find their voices through the transformative power of Poetry Prescribed workshops. As the facilitator of these workshops, I was privileged to witness the incredible growth and the profound catharsis that unfolded week after week.

Within these captivating verses, you will glimpse the raw emotions, the fragmented memories, and the indomitable spirit of these warrior women. From the trembling beginnings of vulnerability to the triumphant declarations of self-worth, these poems encapsulate the journey towards healing and rediscovery. Each word, carefully chosen and crafted, holds the weight of survival, breaking the shroud of silence in which so many victims of abuse find themselves entwined.

Time and again, we gathered, forming a cocoon of trust and mutual support. Through thoughtful discussions, we explored the tangled web of emotions that arise from such trauma. We navigated the labyrinth of self-doubt, slowly but surely, finding solace and strength in one another's stories. And as we gently guided these courageous women through writing exercises, a chorus of voices emerged, hauntingly honest and profoundly beautiful.

In this book, you will encounter the full spectrum of emotions, from the haunting shadows of trauma to the dazzling triumphs of love, hope, and resilience. Each poem is a testament to the self-reclamation that transpired within the workshops as walls crumbled and vestiges of pain were transformed into art. These pages carry the echoes of countless conversations and the whispers of newfound courage.

But perhaps the most extraordinary aspect of these poems lies in their collective power—the power to inspire and uplift others who may still be clawing their way out of the darkest corners of violence. Through sharing their stories with the world, these warrior women extend a lifeline to those who may still feel confined to the shadows, reminding them that they are not alone and that there is strength in unity.

To the readers of this collection, I urge you to read between these lines, to listen to the unspoken stories that echo within these poems. It is my sincerest hope that *Words from Warrior Women* will serve as a beacon of hope, inviting empathy, understanding, and support for survivors of domestic violence everywhere. May these poems instil courage in those who have yet to find their voice, reminding them that their stories deserve to be heard and that healing is possible.

Embrace the raw beauty of these verses, for they are the testament of incredible strength. And as you delve into each carefully woven stanza, may you discover a renewed appreciation for the power of words, the strength of community, and the resilience of the human spirit.

Yours in solidarity,

Esi Yankey
Founder, Poetry Prescribed

Battalion Of Women

I walked many miles in the same beaten shoes,
wondering when the truth might set me free.
I found solace in an empty page and
mapped my way through spilled ink.
Now I use my pen as a torch to
shine a light on the plight of
warrior women who often fight without support,
for this war on women is a cause I can't ignore.
If a pen is a sword,
then I have armed a battalion of women who have since risen from the
depths of pain this book attempts to explain.
This poetry encapsulates the thoughts of women who deserved more,
who channeled their raw emotion into verse translating their experience
into something worth being heard.
So please be kind as you delve into the stories of their lives, and take
some time to listen to another woman's cry.

Miss Yankey
Spoken Word Poet, Facilitator, Activist

PREFACE

We first heard Miss Yankey perform at the Million Women Rise march and rally in London in 2019. In awe of the power of her words and how they meant something to all of us in the audience, I was determined to bring her poetry back to our groups and let everyone share in the feeling of the day. As always when you hear something that sets off so many light bulb moments flickering in your head, it's hard to play it back in all its glory, but then the video of the performance was posted on YouTube and we were able to share those many light bulb moment words in full with our groups. Wow, was the call out, she's speaking about our experiences!

"Do you think Miss Yankey ever comes to Birmingham?" I was asked by a group member. "Could we have a workshop run by her?" Then Covid arrived and with that our base was closed and we all began delivering our services online, and with that came the opportunity to invite Miss Yankey into our project through Zoom. With funding through the West Midlands Police and Crime Commissioner, Miss Yankey led a six-week Poetry Prescribed Course for our groups. Each week with Miss Yankey's lead-ins, the words flew out; lines of anger, pain, injustice but also hope, sisterhood, empowerment and healing. Further sessions were requested and added leading to many more words that needed to be heard.

The theme of Million Women Rise 2019 where we first heard Miss Yankey was "Never Forgotten" ensuring that the women and girls murdered by men would be remembered! Their names, their faces, their lives, their pain.

"We will not be silenced! We will not be forgotten!" were the chants of the day. The poetry produced in this booklet also chants, "We will not be silenced, we will not be forgotten!" Thank you, Miss Yankey, for this wonderful opportunity, for your guidance, your words, your encouragement and your love and kindness to all who participated.

Thank you to all the women who have contributed, came to each session, told their story in verse, opened their hearts so that others might understand and to give hope to other women out there still suffering at the hands of abusive men. Words that might describe how you are feeling; words to encourage you to reach out when you can; (we know reaching out is the hardest step) words to help you know that it's not your fault; to know you have done nothing wrong; and to know that there is nothing wrong with you; words of hope to let you know that healing is possible. We send you love and hugs.

And to you who have downloaded this book, thank you for taking the time to read our poetry. These are our stories, our lives, our pain, our hopes, our survivorship and our thrivership.

In the words of Miss Yankey, "Leaving isn't easy, instead of asking why, please, take some time to listen to another woman's cry."

— **Jacky Mulveen,** *Project Manager, WE:ARE (Women's Empowerment and Recovery Educators)*

***

"Helping women who have suffered abuse, pain and exploitation to find the words to express their experiences truly, their hopes rather than hopelessness, and their power is no small thing. I have worked alongside WE:ARE for over a decade now. They support women and help women find their voices and their power. This is not only done through classic support and social work but through creativity, movement and working with language to challenge what their abusers have taught them to think and say. Language and words are the greatest tools in the abuse of women, they cut harder, sit deeper and poison further than any act of physical violence could. We women must also weaponise words to help us heal and protect ourselves. Years of attending groups at WE:ARE has taught me that women have a common language, secret codes and a way of making language work for us. I can think of no greater tribute to all the women who have suffered and to all the women fighting back in order to thrive than a tribute to our language, our words, our power. The pen is mightier than the sword and a pen wielded by women can change the world forever."

— **Jess Phillips MP,** *Parliamentary Under-Secretary of State in the Home Office.*

***

"What a phenomenal book, a true testimony of strength, light and liberation! I too wrote one of the poems enclosed in this book after attending all of the life-changing WE:ARE programmes, not understanding what was truly possible at that time. Not thinking I was worthy. I have gone on to achieve more than I could have ever imagined, with the support and love of those who have bared their souls in this book. The true warriors, the victors, the change makers. I am now so proud to be an ambassador for this charity, this movement; they changed my life and the life of my children. This book is so powerful, not only filled with heartfelt poetry but life-changing words and actions to inspire."

— **Scarlett Allen-Horton,** *Founder of multi-award winning Harper Fox Search Partners, BBC Apprentice Finalist, Business Partner to Lord Sugar, proud WE:ARE Ambassador.*

***

WELCOME TO WE:ARE
Justice-Seeking Jacky

Welcome,
Come in,
Sit down,
We're so glad that you've found us.
Coffee or tea?

You're not alone here as you can see.
1 in 3 women globally
Experience domestic abuse,
You've no need to explain here,
There's shared experiences
And emotions in the room.

You'll soon
Feel a part of something,
A new belonging,
You'll find your feet
And meet
Others who once felt like you
On their first visit.

Over the weeks and months
There'll be many bumps in the road,
But together we'll carry each other through.
Take your time,
Be kind to the amazing you.

You left when you could.
You're here now and although
You might not think so yet,
You will find your way,
And there will come a day
When you will be welcoming
Other new women with a smile,
And pouring them coffee or tea,
Just you wait and see!

The weeks go on,

And with new awareness
Comes new understanding.
A making sense of your body and mind,
Why you feel a certain way at certain times,
And how you can start to change the way you feel.
Being aware, noticing, breathing, feeling,
A new purpose and meaning.

Reflecting on coping mechanisms once used,
All creative methods of surviving abuse.
Some good, some less so, but
Either way,
They got you through each day
And helped those thoughts go away.
They helped you cope with the pain that's so hard to explain
To others and self.
The emotional distress,
The loneliness.
Ways that helped you avoid abuse and survive just another day,
Just to get by.

You tried.
You may have justified, denied, minimised —
No shame in that, it's how we cope when we feel there's no hope.
But when we remove the toxic person from our life,
The cause of our distress,
We can start to redress the ways we cope.
Find new ways,
More helpful, less stressful ways.

And once you know the hows and the whys,
With the strength and courage to reach out and seek support,
And speak to those who have been there and now thrive,
Feel alive and strive to help others,
You too can join the dots...

And the whys become the 'How can I?' and
The 'What ifs?' become 'Next time...'
'What's next to enjoy?
How can I
Live life to my full potential?

Belong,
Reach goals,
Empower others
In the way I was empowered?'

A pause, a breath, a smile.
Your rights reclaimed,
And so much more gained
That you never allowed yourself to dream of,
To think of,
To let go of.

Sometimes you don't realise
how far you've travelled
Until you look back and then forward again.
You took the right road in the end,
With the help of new-found friends.
You walked through the door.
So many bumps in the road you endured along the way.
You built your new Toolkit,
One tool at a time.
Building blocks,
One step at a time.
One day at a time.

Days turned to weeks, then months.
Movement in feeling, thinking, explaining to others and self.
This new knowledge that was actually there all along,
Just waiting for your moment to shine.
And now your light is shining.
You are the person who shines your light,
Your empowered self.
Your inspirational words.
Your sisterhood on to the next woman who walks in through the door.
And you become the woman who says:

"Welcome,
Come in,
Sit down.
We're so glad that you've found us.
Coffee or tea?"

When Hope Is Gone
Victorious Victoria

When hope is gone,
It still isn't over.
You are not finished yet.
This is not the last page.
You still have the power to act.
You have a hidden super-power called Trust.
Reach out.
There will be someone there
To cut through confusion, despair and panic.
There will be someone with
The humanity and energy to offer you a hand,
A lifeline.
Trust someone.

Indulge Me
Valid Vicky

Indulge me for a moment while I pen a rhyme
To help me express how I feel of the crime,
That us women have lived with, suffered, endured
Behind front doors where we never felt secured.
But we're not looking for pity, we're building a chance
To be free of abuse and bad romance.
We have escaped, but it doesn't stop there
Time now to get empowered, recover, repair.
He comes back, you see, with every trick in the book,
And trauma bonds mean that you cant help but look.
But poetry, spoken word, has an evidence base,
For helping to repair trauma all over the place.
The ancient Greeks identified it, it makes you think,
As under Apollo, healing and poetry have a definite link.
A therapeutic distraction, something bold, something new,
And all the while rebuilding and rediscovering you.
We have laughed, shared, and cried,
Dug down to feelings kept deep inside.
Reflected on sisterhood, looked ahead, looked behind,
And in speaking our truths, some peace we would find.

So my opinion to anyone who thinks poetry is absurd...
Its value reflected in our work and growth, down to every last word.

Impossible Gifts
Warrior Will, a Warrior Woman's son (age 10)

These are the gifts, if I could, I would give to you...
A crystal from a serpent's tail;
A pinch of stardust, from the first ray of golden sun in Spring;
to the last shade of snow in winter,
I search for a mammoth's tusk to bare on the wall;
The dust from the moon, I propose you space;
A diamond from a fish scale;
A feather from a golden winged unicorn;
A lucky horseshoe from the finest horse;
The noise of silence to help you sleep;
The invisible power of an owl's vision,
so you can see for miles.

Let me take you down an ever-ending path of hope
Because, mum, this is for you.

A Breath Of Thankfulness
Justice Seeking Jacky

Again a breath of thankfulness
A moment of goodness
Something done for me
I sit back
How lovely
And just to think
I was never coming back anymore
once I closed that door
Or
Once I put the phone down
Quick plans were always made in my head when that happened
A holiday
A friends reunion
A day trip, a weekend or two

Breathing in the air of spontaneity
Looking forward to a new me
Freedom to wear, share, not care,
No more despair
Walking on sand instead of eggshells
Sleeping on softness instead of a hard place
Opening doors to smiles instead of glares
Watching what I'd like to watch on tv
Eating what and when I'd like to eat
Going to bed at night instead of the early hours
Choosing instead of always pleasing,
Pondering instead of pandering,
Glorious, victorious,
Then ....
The accusing voice reappears
What have I done to him
How could I be so cruel
He had things planned
Dreams to be made
And because of me now ruined
Always ending with 'are we ok now?'
As if nothing had happened
And all back to 'normal'
Then Something nice offered, promised, a mere morsel, but nice none the
less
Again a breath of thankfulness
A moment of goodness
Something done for me
I sit back
How lovely
And just to think
I was never going to come back once I closed that door
Or
Once I put the phone down
Quick plans gone again and again and again and again

She Is Paper
Anon

She is paper, natural woven fibres.
Through earth and dirt she grew,
Where water and light became lovers.
While bending with the wind and reaching to the sun,
She provides haven and life-giving air.
Fluttering branches suggest a delicacy she will deny,
Coarse bark gives a toughness that the leaf tips belie.

She is paper,
Cut her down to size,
She changes form,
But watch new life unfold before your eyes.
You deem her too tall and mighty for your garden,
So fell her;
But don't forget,
Women are not known for inertia.

She is paper,
Going literally through the mill.
Her recipe is of water,
Chemicals and makeup;
Sifted and sorted against her free will.
Shaped by the fight against the mesh of expectation,
Squeezed between tight rolls,
She glides past you in flirtation.

Scrunch her,
Smooth her,
Paint her,
She is paper.

Paper thin and see through,
You trace over her,
Your image of who she is.
You judge her by her cover,
And like the pages of a book,
Her body tells a story;
The marks on her skin are just words printed on a page.

Turn her over,
And when you're done reading,
The page folds in the corner,
Like how she folded in the corner crying rain.

Even as a battered novella with a tired spine,
No matter how many hands touch her,
With pages torn and dirtied,
Her story is all mine

You,
Woman,
Are the message and the medium.
Your pages tell your story
and pronounce your truth.
You are paper and paper is you.

Drop The Disorder!

Justice Seeking Jacky

Dear Psychiatrist, CPN, Doctor and all the others who label us,

How are your labels and meds going to help?
Are they going to stop my abuser being a vile, nasty, cruel and demanding
Bully?
Will they help me manage the situation or shut me down so I can't feel?
The body keeps the score,
so I need to express how I feel,
process how I feel
not push everything down,
hidden away, cos I know it's there, bubbling away
threatening to let rip at any moment.

Are your meds going to stop the rule setting?
list making,
piss taking,
nice guy faking,
women hating bully,
who still expects everything done to his standards whilst we're
breastfeeding, cooking, cleaning,

17

tending to children,
trying to keep a cool exterior to the outside world?

And then you tell us we've got
postnatal depression,
or maybe anxiety disorder,
Borderline Personality Disorder,
take your flippin' pick disorder!
Let me see what I pull out of the hat disorder,
in the DSM book disorder,
and on and on and prescribe even more drugs
on top of the ones that don't work because that's not what we needed.
A chemical imbalance you say??
Let's get it right, it's a power imbalance!
Theories, never queried, just used to abuse us further.

What if we said to you:
"He wants sex just after I've given birth.
He said I'm still fat, ugly, and mad.
He tells me I'm lazy.
He shouts because dinner isn't ready
even though today I've been shopping,
taken kids to school,
cleaned up best I could,
went to the baby clinic,
fed, changed, soothed baby,
cried when baby wouldn't settle,
cried when I wished my family could help;
but he doesn't like them so they can't visit.

Cried when I remembered I have no friends
to speak to because he doesn't like them either,
cried because he told me I was mad,
a crap mother, a useless wife,
cried because I'm starting to believe him,
cried because I dread when he comes in for his dinner
and I know it won't be ready because I'm useless and I can't cope.
And I cried some more because my children
aren't getting the love and support they need
because I'm too damn tired thinking about and seeing to his needs
because if I don't, all hell will break loose.

Oh but I can't cry when he comes home as he hates tears
so that's when I hold it in and it goes to my stomach
and I can't eat because I feel sick.
So there, there's another disorder you can heap on me...
and diagnose IBS on top,
AKA Irritable Bastard Syndrome,
and add more meds!

It really isn't rocket science
and no one even needs a degree,
an O level,
not even a flippin entry level flippin 1 to work out
that instead of PND postnatal depression
I've got a vile, evil, cruel, nasty abuser living in my home
whilst trying to look after my baby.
But maybe...
If you rename PND
Partner's a Narcissist Disorder
then yes I've definitely got PND.
Or Partners a Nob Disorder,
oh I've definitely got that one too!
BPD? Oh yes I've definitely got
Bastard Partner Disorder too,
Now known as
EUPD;
Evil Unreliable Partner Disorder.
No meds will help that.

The only cure is for him to be out of our lives,
To go,
To leave.
He didn't, but we did.
We left,
we're free and guess what?
No more anxiety,
no more isolation,
no more degradation,
no more humiliation,
no more confusion,
low moods, shouting, screaming,
crying, shutting down, withdrawing,

walking on eggshells,
hyper-vigilance,
and not even one tablet has passed our lips!
Not a flippin one!

I repeat over and over the cure was being listened to,
believed and supported.
Shown kindness, hugs, smiles, understanding,
compassionate agencies,
and being able to get away safely.

So Please ask the right questions,
see beyond what we present as,
study coercive control,
it does the most damage,
we can't see it but we can feel it.
Learn from us.
Let us be part of your learning,
support us,
admire our courage,
our determination,
and our passion to make change for us,
our children,
and the next generation.

Drop the disorder!

Dear Doctor

Justice-Seeking Jacky

Dear Doctor,
I can't sleep
I'm feeling suicidal
I suffer with headaches
I'm paranoid all the time
My body aches
I cry for no reason
I'm exhausted
I've got no motivation
I don't want to mix with anyone

I wish I was dead.

"NO",
I want to shout at the top of my voice
it's not depression, postnatal depression,
or this and that disorder.
Why should I be labelled?
All the above are symptoms of abuse,
symptoms of living with an abusive man.

"ASK ME",
I might not tell you straight away as I'm too scared,
but at least I'll know that when I'm ready,
I'll know where I can go.

He's never really hit me
Justice Seeking Jacky

He's never really hit me you know,
Okay, so he puts me down
but then he picks me up again.
He doesn't like my friends,
but that's okay cos yeah,
I suppose he's right cos they're all slags anyway.

He controls all the money,
but then he buys me something nice.
He tells me what to wear,
cos he knows what looks good on me.
He picks the furniture, the colour, the design,
he's got a real flair for that,
While I'm bloody hopeless.
He says I'm a crap cook.
Well I do mess up sometimes,
I mean I burn the occasional dinner,
but that's usually when we're arguing.

He says "I'm a CRAP mum",
oh but you wanna see the lovely flowers
he brought me for mothers day.

We'd probably had a row the night before,
that's when I normally get flowers.
I actually can't remember if we rowed or not.
Maybe we did, maybe we didn't,
cos he says I imagine things, maybe I do.
He says I should be grateful that he puts up with me,
that no one else would –
especially now I've let myself go.
He doesn't like me in make-up you see,
says I shouldn't waste my money at the hairdressers,
tells me he loves me just the way I am.

He even made a doctor's appointment for me,
he's caring like that.
Told me not to tell the doctor private stuff though.
He's right, they're all bloody nosy in that surgery.
"Just say you can't sleep and you're sad and crying all the time for no reason.
He'll hand out some pills that'll cure your depression."
I couldn't believe it at the surgery when the doctor asked me
if I was suffering from Domestic Violence.
I said, "he's never really hit me you know."

Being A Woman
Lovely Laura

Being a woman means vulnerability in the wrong hands.
Superwoman when allowed to flourish,
I have crawled through the heinous swamp of a narcissist's mind.
I have walked over the lines.
I have always lived by a higher power.
I have run from the silent misery I was trapped in.
I have overcome the cruellest heartbreak while trying to pursue my ultimate dreams.
I never stopped achieving.
Being a woman means resilience and strength.

I'm Free!
Outstanding Obi

Who am I?
> What am I doing?
>> Where is my life headed?

I only said yes to love,
Not to this feeling of the weight of the world on my shoulders.

Alone in mourning,
My visions,
Abandoned.
The unfulfilled desires,
Broken promises.

Empty.
Defeated.
Perplexed.

Have I done this?
> Did I choose this?
>> Have I earned this?

>> Where do I go from here?
> What do I tell our seedlings?
How do I ignite my fire?

I depended on you.
Shit.

How do I decide?
> How do I live?

They say it's a man's world,
But you left mine so I guess it's my world.

One step at a time.
Learning and growing.
Standing on the shoulders of warrior women,
Who are kings in their world!

Masters of their lives!!

Owning my life,
Finding me.
Learning to live,
To love,
To breathe without your permission.

I'm fucking free!!!

Not Your Usual Fairytale
Valid Vicky

The fairytale starts all shimmering and gold,
But something went awry,
Jane doesn't do as she's told.
"You have to do this,
You mustn't do that,
And God help you if you try to get out of that flat."

It seems perplexing,
It seemed absurd,
"Oh no I've shacked up with a right bleedin' turd."
Realisation,
He treats her worse than a dog,
It turns out that her prince was actually a frog.

One night with back-up Jane grew her own balls,
And left him– the turdman,
And blocked all his calls.
And now warrior women from far and from near,
Show up to ensure a fresh start doth appear.

It sure wasn't easy,
Perseverance and stealth,
But we'll make sure you again love yourself.
Of the prince you may ask,
Well I am told he was left all alone,
And out in the cold.

Learning What You Are
Valid Vicky

The way you treated me made me hurt,
I spiralled into confusion and searched for answers in voids of sadness.
The yin and yang of one minute bombing me with love,
And the next minute shooting me down with your hateful words.
The pain.
The shame.
The feeling in my gut like I had been punched,
Although you did not need to use your fists.
My yearning to understand,
To make sense of the nonsense.
The madness.
The foulness.
Don't let them see,
Don't let them hear.
The shame.
Just pain,
No gain.

I'm angry that I accepted it.
Angry that my children saw it.
I'm angry.
You didn't need to do that.
Say that.
Smash that.

You had me and I loved you deeply.
Nobody would have taken me from you.
I told you,
Told you,
Told you that you were the only one
Who could drag me away from you.

And you pushed,
Shoved 'til we broke.
And now I'm healing.
Feeling.
Not reeling from the fights anymore.
Learning what you are,

That it was you and never was me.
Learning I'm not the one for you
And we just weren't to be.

Drive My Heart Into A Ditch
Lovely Laura

Picked up,
      Dropped.
Picked up,
      Dropped.
Picked up,
      Dropped.
Picked up,
      Dropped.

How much more can I take?
You know my heart has stopped.
You continue regardless,
Bleeding me dry,
Filling my head with more lies.

I'm not good enough,
      I'm stupid,
            I'm a child,
                  I'm a joke.

But you're happy when I'm not woke to what you're really doing here.
Filling me with fear,
The next time you're going to disappear and come back,
Keeping me stuck in this fucking trap.

I feel dead inside,
      My body and mind,
             His toy...

His playground when he feels like messing around.

He knows I'll be down,
For his ploy to be a man,

But he's nothing but a damaged little boy.

Hooked to Youtube videos explaining narcissistic abuse,
But what's the use?
The noose never loosens,
The pain I feel from knowing it was all a scam.
Years of my life down the drain,
One big plan.

Woman
Outstanding Obi

Yeah, actions speak louder
So loud that it quakes with every pound
I woman reduced to a hole
Meet for your key
Yeah, and I one of many too,
Perplexed that you think
I would lie still and take the beating
I found my words, I'm not backing down!
Roll over, the head has been activated
No cunt definitely not for a while
Till your actions become deserving of
My beauty to bestow

Spoken Word
Outstanding Obi

I sit and ponder
did I do right, can I say no
I sit and wonder
Do I go on, can I get off now?
I sit and banter
Do it, let's go, see now you did it!
I keep my fears inside
I keep them well hidden
Behind the layers of powder
I keep the tear behind the mascara
Look, I keep my mind sane

By keeping the pain deep in me

The code to my heart I cannot decode
Was there ever a code, shall I ever be free from this fail?
The code to my future is in my progress my learning,
It's left to me, not him, my code to find
When I'm not here I am there somewhere
Soaring far far away in the beautiful
country fields built for only me
When I'm not here I find me there
Lost but not in my world where pain is not.

My mind is beautiful deep wide
My mind has layers and layers that I may never find
My mind is on its journey to healing me

Sometimes I cry
sometimes I smile
Sometimes I laugh but

Most times I long for a day When the light shines bright on me
Sometimes I might learn to love but now
Let me alone for a time

Would you judge me if
You knew all there was
Would you judge me if I was truly yours
Would you judge me if I threw it all away
15 years in 15 seconds
Would you judge me if you were in my shoes?

I cannot find the words to express how truly I feel
My mouth opens to see all I have said in my head
But I can't find the words to see what I must
The beautiful thing is the sound of Aiah's laughter
The beautiful thing is Sam's fair eyes
The yawn of Manny when his tummy needs a feeding
The loud thud of Danny's feet as he storms to do his chores
And Nate's cry for Mama

Freedom means access to help when I need

Access to wealth I have slaved for
Freedom means succeeding at being the boss of me
Freedom means a roof over my head shoes on my soles

Fortress
Fabulously Fearless

From death's door,
I nursed you back to health.
Every hour God sent,
Working to earn money you spent.

Your mortgage,
Your bills,
Your food,
Your treachery and lies,
Were all paid for by my hard-working hands.

You continued to fake being sick
So you could continue to leach from someone.
So consumed with worry and guilt,
That I could not see you for the parasite that you are.
I gave you the best of me;
My love,
My trust.

My body grew four miracles,
And even though you watched me bring them
Into the world full of anguish and pain,
You belittled my achievement
And focused on how tired you were.

You bled me dry for years and years;
My withered and tired soul could take no more,
But still you bullied,
Cajoled,
Coerced,
And controlled.

When that didn't destroy me,

You chose to hurt my babies.
But that was your fatalistic mistake my friend,
Because you forced me to unleash the lioness in me.
Your pain I endured,
But my babies could not,
Would not,
Not if I had anything to do with it.

Little by little,
Step by step,
Day by day,
This lioness has emerged fully grown.

No more bullshit,
No more lies,
Your pathetic presence has been completely wiped clean,
We have erased you from our lives,
And soon from our memories too.
I have rebuilt this fortress,
And I will guard it with my recovered and nurtured soul,
You will never darken this threshold again.

For three years I've stumbled and striven
To find a place I can finally call my own.
In the depth of darkness and despair,
There has always been a glimmer,
The tiniest of shimmers that held within its grasp,
A beacon of light,
A light so bright,
It will blind you.

A force so strong,
I had no choice but to allow its strong warm embrace
To lead me along this path,
Where I could finally breathe a sigh of relief,
Take a seat and ponder the truth I've hidden,
Locked away so long that I no longer recognised it as my very own.

Finally I could bare my soul for all to see,
It was not me,
It was that hidden in plain sight enemy

That had taken everything I was and turned it to stone.
Now I'm free of the burdens of the past,
You want to question what I have found?

I found ME!!!
I am bold,
I am beautiful,
But more importantly,
I am FREE!

Who Am I?
Fabulously Fearless

Who am I?
I keep searching and questioning...
Who am I?

I keep searching,
Trying to remember where I saw myself last
To help me remember who I am.

I used to be whole,
But somewhere I lost my soul.
You thought you could destroy me,
But you didn't know that like a phoenix,
I will rise from the ashes of your lies,
Burning so bright that it blinds your eyes.

I am water,
Calm and still,
I am the gentle breeze.

I am the crashing waves,
A tornado and hurricane,
I am the eagle soaring high above the mighty mountains.

I dance in the rain and paint with rainbows,
I swim in the deepest oceans
And have everything within me that I need to thrive.

That door that was once open to you,
The door that you smashed down,
Crashed through,
Will be open no more.
It is now barred shut,
And what is more,
I've taken back the keys;
And by doing so have freed myself.

I am finally free to be who I want to be.
Like an elf I'm putting you back on the shelf,
And there you will stay forever and a day!

We Remember
Strong Sammie

Sometimes in the darkness we remember the walls closing in,
We remember the nights of horror,
the days of torment all from someone we thought of as kin.
Remembering the hot breath on your neck,
that cold touch of pain and nothing in return but a peck.
It's okay to remember
but what we need to remember now,
Is that we can turn the light on!

You Will Find Me Here
Anon

I sit where I am and cannot move.
I'm made of stone,
             Of brick,
                       Of wood.

You tried to drag me,
             Cut me,
                       Ruin me.
I did not move.

I am here.

I keep my memories like secrets because I don't know if they are true.
How did I live that way?

How did I survive?

Why did I stay?

I don't know myself in this place,
The songs keep on,
And the truth bleeds out of the speaker.

Loud and cryptic.

The code to my heart is lost,
No one knows it,
Only my son can enter,
I can't even enter myself.

He goes where I cannot,
Where no one else can ever visit,
He lives there.
Through him I love myself.

When I'm not here I cry,
I escape but I cry,
The body is vulnerable away from this space,
Cold and lost.

Who can find me,

I'm lost.

Only I.

Cold and wet woods hide my body,

Tears,
Pain.

My mind is my own.
I fucking own it,
I took it back,
You tried it didn't you?
You really fucking tried it;
But I snapped and took it back.

No one will take my mind again.
Sometimes I forget how close to the edge I was,
But just know I will hold on now for life.

My sanity,
      My rock,
            My sanctuary is me.

Would you judge me if I told you I have no time for your judgments?
That I don't care what you think?
I can't find the words to explain my mindset,
But I'm here,
      I'm free,
            And no one will ever take me again.

There is no backing down,
            No letting go.
                  The beautiful thing is my freedom,
                         My hurriya,
               Oh how we don't know it 'til we lose it.
          Wandering ignorant,
And chained up without realising.

Freedom means weightlessness,
        Responsibility for myself,
            Making mistakes,
               Living.

I am here and I love it.
You will find me here.

It Is Not Your Right

Lily

It is not your right to bully me.
      It is not your right to dictate what I can watch on TV.

It is not your right to tell me what I can wear.
      It is not your right to forget my birthday and say you don't care.

It is not your right to belittle me and call me names.
It is not your right to gaslight me with your mind games.

It is not your right to molest me whenever you feel.
It is not your right to make me ill.

It is not your right to be waited on hand and foot.
It is not your right to tell me how I need to look.

It is not your right to wake me up to pleasure you.
It is not your right to cut me off so I withdrew.

It is not your right to chain me to the kitchen.
It is not your right to kill my ambition.

It is not your right to keep me financially dependent.
It is not your right to blame me for your constant discontent.

It is not your right to shout in my face.
It is not your right to invade my personal space.

It is not your right to kick me in the head.
It is not your right to punch my pregnant belly,
and tell me you hope my baby is now dead.

It is not your right to keep me from living.
It is not your right to take constantly emotionally and never be giving.

It is not your right to keep me from family and friends.
It is not your right to have that attitude that condescends.

It is not your right to steal my life.
It is not your right to own your wife.

It is not your right to get away scot-free.
It is not your right to completely break me.

It is my right to take ownership of my life and my future.
It is my right to get away from you, my abuser.

Anger
Lovely Lucy

I got told,
If you want to detach,
You need to find the memory of your attachment.
I'm sitting here with this hurt,
Wondering what meaning I have given to this hurting pain.
All I can remember is when we sat together,
You told me you cheated on me,
But that wasn't all,
She was pregnant.
My world of 15 years together came crashing down,
My body shook,
My limbs were shaken,
My throat choked up,
Worse than before when you laid your hands around my neck,
What a fucking disaster.

Anger took over.
Why?
How?
Where?
All he did was blame the drugs,
Her,
Then me,
Like I forced him to commit adultery.
I just sit with my anger,
Locate it in my body,
Talk to it because it's a gift,
How would I know when you do me wrong
If it never stuck by my side?
Each predator would lead you to your death,
That leash around your neck,
Oh I thank my anger.
You are my friend,
You lead me to have boundaries,
When to give a big fuck you,
A golden middle finger.

Now you're gone,

My peace arrived,
That peace of mind.
I lock my door each night not wondering,
If you're coming home,
Or who you're fucking.
I lie back and listen to my meditation,
Oh what a life!
I can breathe and exhale that love,
Divinely embedded into my heart.
I can feel myself,
My soul.
All I need right now is me,
I give myself to me,
No one else.
I am light,
I am love,
I am whole,
This is who I want to be,
A free bird, who is doing me.

Pain Reflected
Anon

Sometimes you have to travel alone
And take a deep breath in as you step into the cold.
Fill your lungs so you know you're alive.

I fly blind and rely on the hot wind's rise.
Elevation of thought,
Body and power,
Watch me be taken away from you.

My thoughts are my limits,
So free my mind,
Dust away the cobwebs from all corners.

Sometimes I get lost and my compass broken,
My map worn…
I feel dark and take shelter
But I know the light will return.

I tried to warn you,
This is my growth,
How I achieve speed,
Solace.
I am serenity,
Synced with strength,
Surrounded by sun.

Pain held a mirror to what I could be
And I rejected those options and chose differently.

This was a new kind of day,
I awoke to darkness and the sun rose at night.
Taking my time,
I drew the curtains back.

I discovered me in the cracked window.
Tired eyes saw who I was becoming in spite of it all.

I thought that I was spent and in debt,
But that was their voices talking shit they did not know.

Here I am again looking in the window.
Vague reflection,
A view out to the world and how I reach my hand to open.

Lesson Of A Lifetime
Lovely Laura

I'm angry at what he's done and what I've become.
Undone,
I run far away to the sea,
Taking shelter under the sun.
I'm healing from all that I'm left reeling from.

You were just a joke,
Absolute scum,
Having me on my knees,
Happy to receive breadcrumbs.
Punished,

Shamed,
Humiliated for being in this state,
When it was you that put me here in the first place.

No acknowledgement of your part in all of this,
The old me I really miss,
You disabled me and walked into the abyss.

Well, I finally got my answer,
Never sorry,
No change,
Business as usual,
Everything is the same.

It broke my heart,
But now I know I need to go.
The grief process is giving me peace,
Knowing I just need to go with the flow
I hope one day these emotions and the horror will fade,
I've even started to pray.
My heart feels closed forever.
The thought of another makes me queasy,
You've made my life so mind-bleedingly uneasy.
Thank you for teaching me the lesson of a lifetime,
But it was too much and too prolonged,
The trauma bond was strong.
Finally, set free from where I never belonged.

He Fooled You, Too
Justice Seeking Jacky

He signed up for a weekend Anger Management course,
It was to show the courts he'd changed his ways.
Wow, that tutor deserves a medal
If he believes he can change a lifetime of beliefs in just 3 days!
They all praised him to the highest heavens for doing oh so well,
He'd conned them all as usual, but I was still going through hell.
But they ticked their boxes and gave him a smile
When he told them how it had been all worthwhile.
That charming, manipulative man of mine
will pull the wool over you every time.

They're clever like that, in complete control you see,
He's tricked you the same way he tricked me.
At least now I know that I'm not so stupid, and it's not all my fault
As he also managed to fool you, the Judge in the Family Court.

When England Plays
Fabulously Fearless

Today I cheered,
First one goal,
Then another.
Hold your breath until full-time,
The whole country is on tenterhooks
waiting for the final whistle to blow.
They say the reporting of domestic abuse
Skyrockets after England plays,
Please win,
Don't lose, they pray.

All those women locked indoors
With monsters who need an excuse to start.
"Nah, don't be silly, that's not true.",
Oh yes it is,
I've lived it since the World Cup in 2006.
From watching and supporting every international event,
To hiding my disgust and shame for anything done in England's name.

He didn't drink,
He didn't have that to blame.
He used his privilege and entitlement because that was his game.
Today I watched eating popcorn,
Laughing and joking with the trophies I brought into the world.
Today I breathed a sigh of relief because we'd won the game
But deep down I know lots of women won't feel the same.

45

Looking For The Rainbow On A Rainy Day
Notable Naomi

It's been a cold, dark, wet day.
So dismal and the only warmth looking out of the train window was the rainbow that followed my journey with hope of a break in the clouds for the sun to shine through.

Gosh so hard were those days, months, years.
My creativity was grasped in any moment I had free.
Whatever came to mind on the day.
Sometimes singing at the top of my lungs and bashing the notes on the keyboard in a bid to smother the pain that grew inside.
Then looking down at my children and feeling the love grow in so many ways, only to be silenced the moment the back door opened.
In knitting the first dress for my newborn daughter I became totally absorbed in creating something beautiful and so it continued
So happy, yet so sad.
Sometimes sat in the corner of the smallest kitchen, head in hands.
Exasperated, lost, hollow.
Questioning ...How to break free with nowhere to go.
The dreams were never a reality to me at the time, just a distant hope.
Then Creativity would sweep in once again unearthing a mound of daisies the one year which have now evolved to where they dance around in their freedom of today.

My early daisies being my escape, my hope for freedom.
However at the time not really grasping the true meaning of the flowers that flourished around me in my paint and mind.
Now being my reality where the rainbow stands forth smothering the last drops of rain from the storm that billowed over my life when I wore the ring that trapped me in time.
Creativity now dips in and out of the storms of moving on, making new life.
Creating new paths.
When the pen doesn't dance on my page
Words at times spring to mind , being bottled with other words collected over years.
Keeping creativity alive and raring to go.
Every last drop combining, enriching and healing my broken soul into

something beautiful, to share, to encourage others that there is hope when freedom calls.

Sometimes
Fabulously Fearless

Sometimes you have to travel alone on this journey we call life.
Many people may join you, but they won't be able to stay for long.

I fly blind most of the time;
My heart is the window to my soul and of this truth I am sure.
My thoughts are often chaotic,
They jump and flit like butterflies in the sun,
Soaring high in the sky.

Sometimes I get lost in a certain pattern of thought
But sometimes I find myself for sure;
Hidden under the debris of everyday life.

I tried to be who they wanted me to be
But they still shook their heads and clucked their tongues;
Their standards I would never attain.
So I've shaken off the shackles of their heavy lies
And I'm free to be whoever I want to be.

Pain held a mirror to the depths of my soul.
Now I know there can be rainbows with just a little rain,
I have no need for their hurricane.

This was a new kind of beauty to me;
This being free.
I danced and I sang,
I walked and I ran.
From the depths of despair to the joys of freedom.

I discovered me, as if by accident.
But there she was,
Hidden all along;
Waiting to come back out and share herself with me.
Her silliness and giggles lighting up the room once more;

She's no longer afraid or ashamed.

I thought that I was destined to be angry and alone.
Little did I know that my rage and misery would find a home
With loving hearts and souls who understood and had lived the same pain.

I am no longer afraid to be who I want to be.
I am no longer afraid to own all parts of me;
The good, the bad, the happy and the sad.
I am no longer afraid to own my truth,
And I will no longer hide my truth.

Bored Angry Woman
Anon

Let me just say that I am a very bored person.
I am bored of your predictable bullshit, I saw you coming,
But I'm tired of having to be on the lookout for your kind.
I roll my eyes when you begin the script you brothers learned by heart.
I'm so angry, feeling full of nerves, your true colours sharpen as the image develops.
I'm mad at the reliability of your fuckery coming through like clockwork.
I'm pissed off that you want to be on that team.
I hate that you get to act without questioning as you deny, hide and minimise it all.
I'm mad at the government for not catching rapists.
I'm mad at the media for elevating rapists,
And believe it or not, I'm still pissed off about my childhood – my girlhood...
At 37 I can count the wrong forever.
I'm mad because I've had to suffer the same as so many others.
I'm not special for going through this, my stories, my fears, my scars do not make me unique.
I have every right to be angry but most of the time,
despite what you believe, I am really, really just tired of this shit.

I Believed Because...
Justice Seeking Jacky

Because of the accusations and blame
I believed I was the cause of his abuse
Because of the constant criticism
I believed that I was at fault
Because of the daily put downs
I believed I was worthless
Because of the threats
I believed I had to do as I was told
Because of the isolation
I believed I had no support
Because he always said he was sorry
I believed that he was
Because he bought me flowers
I believed I should forgive him
Because he said the children needed a dad
I believed they would be upset without him
Because he said I was a bad mother
I believed I couldn't cope on my own
Because he said I was depressed
I believed I was mentally ill
Because he accompanied me to the doctors
I believed he cared

Because I saw a poster in the surgery about domestic violence
I believed that might be why I was depressed
Because I somehow found the strength to call the number
I believe that is why I am here today to tell the tale
Because I was listened to and believed
I believed I was not to blame
Because I made that call
I believed in the support I was offered
Because of that support
I now believe in myself
I deserve the right to live free from fear and abuse.

Channelling Rage
Lucious Luci

Oh how you sit there cracking a joke,
With a spliff in one hand
And a drink in another,
The entitlement is unreal.
You spit words of hate
Detrimental to my health.
The lies roll out your fucking mouth,
Telling me pathetic stories,
All that future faking,
Trying to bond me harder,
Keep me like a property.
You think I'm just bricks, cement and water,
I have a heart. You're a fucking monster,
You ain't nothin' but a predator.

I may be a forgotten woman to your dilemma,
But I will tell you,
I am a woman with honour,
This armour ain't no match for your deluded karma.
Yes that karma will strike you,
Hit you hard.
I ain't coming back.
You are a distant memory,
You are that joker in my pack of cards
Locked away forever,
So do what you want,
You loser.

I Am A Very Patient Person
Valid Vicky

Let me just say that I am a very patient person, but I'm tired of this fight.
Why do we have to teach them how to treat others right?
Sarah Everard, you raped and killed her, was it with a knife?
Who the fuck are you to think you've the right to take a life?
Don't tell me no-one knew that something wasn't right,
Those sexist jokes, entitlement or out to prey at night.

51

Someone saw something, must have through the years,
And just like with Harold Shipman we've got to start acting on our fears.
Share with relevant people, record stuff, get it logged.
Before another woman is a victim to be blogged.
They'll soon come out of the woodwork, people will say they knew,
But why the hell did they stay quiet 'til their fear came true?
And I'm angry that they still pull their fucking vans over to try and talk to school-girls,
And I'm pissed off that girl guides need to walk in pairs in the light of day.
And I'm sick to my stomach that so many women
endure lives of abuse at the hands of their partners.
I'm mad at myself for not telling of the things we saw on our dinner break at school.
And I hate that this problem seems to be here to stay.
I'm mad at the media for perpetuating sexist points of view,
And the lack of action by the government seems shocking and untrue.
I have every right to be angry, but most of the time,
despite what you believe, I am a really, really calm person.

Justice! What Justice?!
Anon

He slapped me in the face, you slapped him on the wrist.
Let back out to torture me, I was just another name on your list
Soon to be filed away, only classed as "standard risk.'
Please see the bigger picture, the abuse does not stop here,
I wasn't seen as a priority but I was still living in fear.
No evidence? What do you want to see?
Broken bones? What about my sanity?
Broken homes, broken souls, broken minds?
That's what his legacy left behind.
Who is this CPS that decides our fate?
How many more times can they make a fatal mistake?
And who decides my risk, standard or high?
And who believes the abusers' obvious lies?
I'm lucky I had some backup support,
That's where I finally got my protection,
Learned what my choices were,
And that I had another option.
Empowered, more knowledgeable,

I have taken back my power.
The project was there for me,
In what I feared might be my final hour.

Don't Judge Me
Justice Seeking Jacky

Agencies please don't judge me
and make me feel any worse than I already feel
Or I won't come back,
and I'll get lost in the system like so many others.

I didn't want this life for me and my children,
I didn't know my knight in shining armour had a deep hidden past.
The services did though,
Probation knew,
Police knew,
Social services knew,
Mental health knew.

With a pat on the back he was free to wound another family.
He's done his time, now I'm left to do mine.

While he moves on to another vulnerable mum,
Whose life will be changed by a man so deranged,
and no one will know until her tears start to flow
and she becomes another statistic.

Still Confused
Valid Vicky

I sit at this stop on my journey,
Healing with a new sense of self.
I keep battling with decisions I've taken,
But I must do this for my own mental health.
The code to my being has been disrupted,
Values so opposing, it's untrue.
But when I'm not here,
I can't help but wish

That things had worked out with you.
But my mind is made up,
There is no going back,
Sometimes I feel foolish that I followed your track.
Would you judge me if you knew the thoughts I had?
I can't find the words to explain how good things were,
Whilst also being so bad.
The beautiful thing is that we tried 'tho we failed.
Freedom means keeping going,
Moving forwards,
And leaving behind those tracks that we trailed.

I Have Every Right To Be Angry
Lovely Laura

Let me just say that I am an outraged person.
I might come across sweet,
But that's because the real me has been beat.

I am flattened, personality dampened.
I realise now how this happened
Inner child, lost in the wild.

But I'm tired of the lies,
What flies in this world.
Conditioned to accept wrong doings,
When clearly it's all wrong.

I'm so angry I implode,
My body is a vessel filled with all it can hold.
Until I'm sick.
I'm mad that what I can't see
Ends up festering inside of me.
I'm pissed off that my nervous system has to shut down,
Just to keep going without showing a frown.

I hate that people tell me to stop obsessing.
How can I when my brain is just processing what it's been fed?

I'm mad at the government for making this life impossible.

I'm mad at the media for creating fantasies which are unattainable.
And believe it or not,
I'm still pissed off that with all this,
I'm supposed to look hot.

I'm mad because I've had to suffer
The illogical realities of our world,
Coming together in support groups for shelter and understanding,
Connection.

I have every right to be angry,
But most of all, despite what you believe,
I just want to be happy and at peace.

Love Doesn't Equal Pain
Anon

Love doesn't equal pain.
Why does he call you those names?
Being in love shouldn't equal pain.
Love isn't how much you suffer,
You're responsible for how you treat another.
Real love lifts you up, makes you feel 10 feet tall,
Not something that makes you curl up in a ball.
Why are you on the floor crying like a child,
while you're carrying his child?
Love doesn't make your soul feel defiled.

Emotional Pain
Lovely Laura

Soul destroyed,
No bruises to show for the insidious destruction in my mind.
Having to have a well-being session explaining how the brain works,
How your behaviour seized up my system.
What the fuck has happened to me,
While he's completely unaffected.

Inflicting pain on my brain,

Long-term damage.
You took advantage,
I trusted you and now I realise I was scammed.
The pain is so horrible,
It doesn't let me rest,
I will never forget.

He thinks no-one will ever know but I know,
You thought I was too stupid to know myself.
Walking away with no shame,
Having zero knowledge of my aftermath.
The audacity of the blatant lies,
King of the Castle asshole,
I hope you rot and cry with no-one to help you,
So you know the pain you've stuck in my system.

Solitary
Outstanding Obi

Breathe, Laura, breathe
As I sit in solitude
Reflecting on a decade and a half
Spent confined, abused, neglected
By the one I chose in love for love
Betrayed but not defeated
Truth is I have had a decade and a half pause
To grow into this strong warrior woman, birthing my release!
My release, is to succeed in life, in work, in body and in mind
Breathe, Laura, breathe

Release Me
Fabulously Fearless

Release me from my solitude.
I can't breathe and my reflection is screaming,
"Release me!!"
Why won't you release me?
So that I can speak more truthfully?

Buffet Of Shame
Anon

Too fat, too thin, too slutty, too prim,
You've danced the line like a music note about to change key.
Stick insect in a jar, here's your nourishment of green.
The square virgin is simultaneously, reality is absent/obscene.
Changed metabolic rate betrays your trust,
now you are growing into a stranger.
Rolls and lumps greet you,
desperate to get to know you while your mum tries to disown you.
Obsessive calorie counting triggers those addictive traits
and you starve your feelings to gain control.
A buffet of shame and lust is in front of me today
and I don't know who to choose.
Comfort? Hunger? Passion? Loneliness?
The only thing I know is who is in the mirror.

Lost Home
Lovely Laura

I am 9 years old,
Everyone saying my name,
Hugging me goodbye.
I get to go on a plane,
I am filled with adrenaline.
As I drive to the airport,
My mum looking over her shoulder,
I am curious as I wake up,
Looking out of the plane window,
I see misty meadows and rain drops.

I am fearful as I meet my stone-faced aunt and uncle,
Quietly loading the car with our suitcases.
I am shy as the drive to their home feels awkwardly silent.
I am uncomfortable, as I see my mum's discomfort.
I am confused as I ask my mum if I should put on a British accent from now on.
I am attention seeking as I try to befriend my cousins who are cold towards me.

I am crying as I ask my Grandma,
"When will I see my dad again?".
I can't ask my mum.
It will upset her more.

I am at school singing hymns I don't understand
in a black, bleak uniform,
As my Californian tan fades.
I am scorned for speaking with an American accent and told,
"Go back to your own country, American bitch".

I am angry,
I dye my hair red,
Listen to Slipknot and smash my bedroom door off its hinges.
I am in trouble now,
I'm handcuffed and shouted at.
I feel like I'm in a black hole.

I emerged as me at age 22.
Finally safe,
My own place to live,
An education I want,
Filled with hope for the future.
My childhood a miserable blur,
I keep going in pursuit of the right path

Minimising – Am I Real?
Anon

You minimised me over and over. You said you forgot.
You forgot? You what?!
I feel invisible.
Am I even here?
If I speak, who will hear me?
If I tell, who will believe me?
You rewrote history, actions reframed to sanitise what happened.
I second guess myself.
I have to remind you what you said,
I have to fight to be seen as human because to you, I don't matter.

People need to know that she can't always find the words,
So he gets in there first and she remains unheard.

His charm, his innocence, no one would believe me anyway.
I struggle to believe it myself.
We don't have the words for this.
I didn't know it was abuse until weeks, months after,
You never accepted it.

Judgement Awaits
Fabulously Fearless

Sitting here waiting to see what judgement awaits,
Keeping my children safe is my crime.
They don't hear what we have to say,
Our voices lost and broken,
The same old lies being peddled as truth.
I raised my voice louder in order to make them hear.
Our voices are louder but the deaf never hear.
So now I must lower my voice and change the language I speak,
So that those sitting in judgement must sit up to deny no longer,
What's always been staring at them in plain sight.

Our need to be heard matters.
Our need for safety matters.
Our need to live in peace matters.
Our freedom,
Our desires,
Our lives,
They matter.

Exhausted.
Tired of thinking.
Thinking about you,
What you did;
Who you were.
This stranger that I married.

"For better, for worse"?
I gave you the best of me,

And in return you gave me your worst.
I gave you my joy and optimism,
You crushed it into the dirt.
I gave you my care,
Love and support,
But got none in return.

I was strong though,
And because you were weak
You had to bring me down.
You had to break me.
You almost did.
But my fire refused to die.
The ember that I kept hidden from you,
It sputters every now and then,
but then it catches with renewed strength.

It will grow and you will not notice
Because you won't be here to enjoy its warmth.
This is not a destructive malicious blaze,
But a warming, welcoming fire;
And you are not invited to sit by it.

I sit and wonder "Where will we go?",
I keep looking back and then I'm lost.
Keep looking forward.
The code to my future lies ahead,
Not behind.
Keep moving forward,
One step at a time.

When I'm not here,
I must remember that here
Is the only place that's real.
Right here,
Right now.

My mind is a maze,
Full of adventures and dead ends.
Sometimes I wish I could go back,
Right back to before it began.

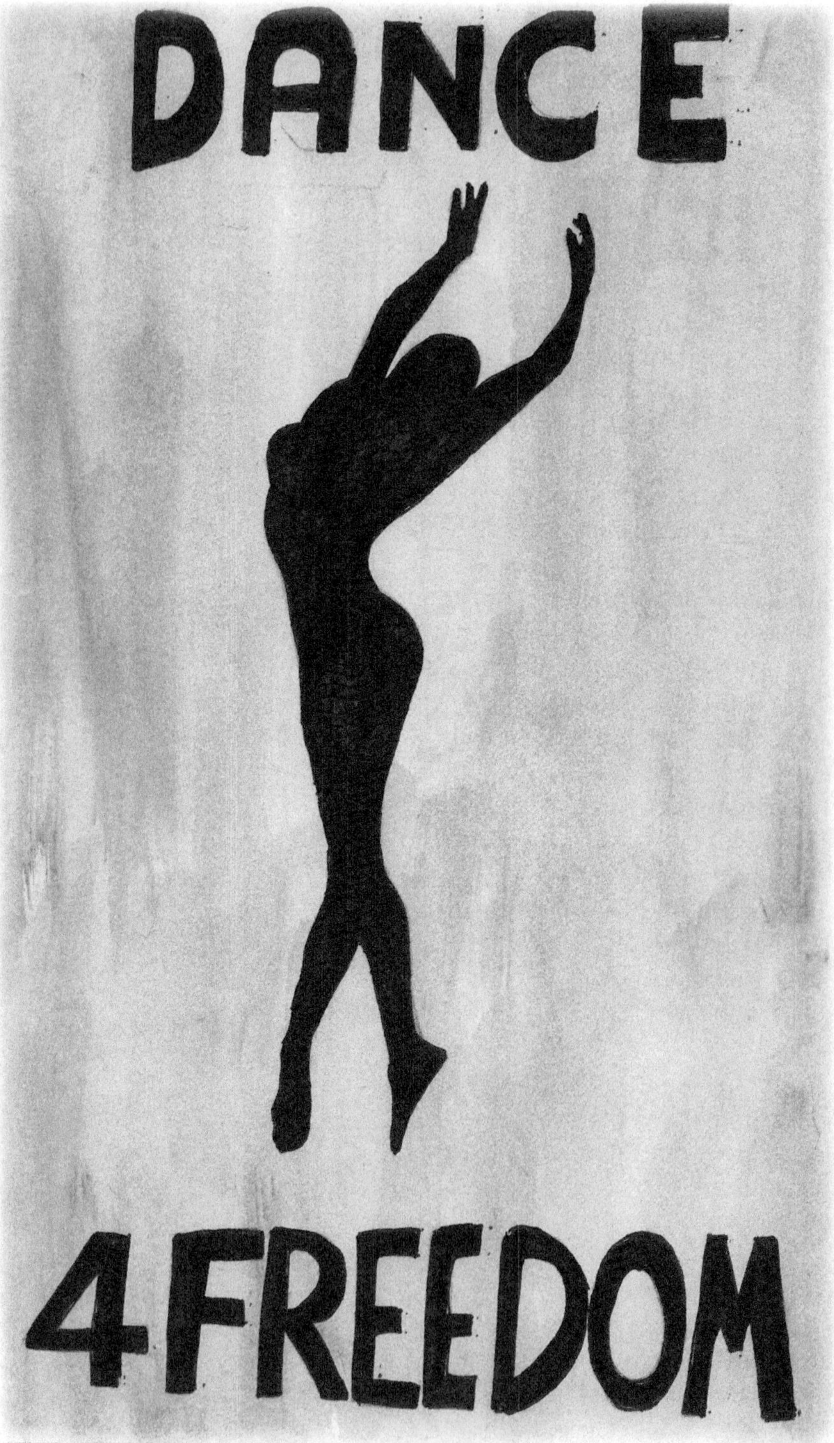
DANCE
4FREEDOM

Would you judge me if you knew the things
I wish I could say and do?
I can't find the words to tell you
How I wish I could change
What's already come to pass.

The beautiful thing is,
Even if I could change it,
I wouldn't go back and erase it.

Freedom means I get to choose.

I Am
SMA

I am here not listening and rushing.
I am working busy and blinkered.
I am wasteful with life not giving you time.
I am hearing those words and regretting while I drive.
I am running through the door praying I'm wrong.
I am looking on watching them working on you,
I am sorry.
I am wanting to help you desperately,
I am sorry.
I am listening to their words, that they will keep trying,
I am sorry.
I am thinking what would you do, stop wasting resources, I am gone.
I am sorry, but they carry on.
I am numb.
I am sorry.
I am thinking what to do to be strong like you would do,
I am sorry.
I am shocked, they ask us what they should do with you,
I am sorry.
I am cuddling you like we always use to do,
I am sorry but I need to protect you,
I am sorry I should have listened to you,
I am sorry I should have given you time.

Blameless
Limitless Lorraine

Who the fuck was to blame?
I know she'd blame me.
I stayed out all night you see,
Took no responsibility.
Responsibility!
Now there's a fucking word indeed.

It was his responsibility not mine;
He was the bastard in disguise!
He was the liar!
He held the power!
His aspersions cast upon my truth.
She was supposed to be on my side,
But to her, they were excuses,
Fucking excuses!
To him a fantasy.
She thought I was disgusting
And just couldn't see the deplorable act he committed on me.
Yet here I was futile,
Fragmented, her 'baby girl' in tatters on the floor.

Mr. Memory
Anon

You don't even have to make excuses if you reduce it down to nothing.
It's not there, what am I complaining about?
You don't have to face what you did if I can't speak about it.
You claim you forgot, you forgot, you what?!
Oh, Mr. Memory, man your brain failed you there.
Next, let's deny what happened.
You'll accept this but not that; it wasn't that bad.
I abused you, but I'm not an abuser.
My voice is gone, my reality is stolen, but I won't be powerless forever.
We see through your tactics, our eyes are open.
We hold up a hand to say stop — as we take back our truth.

What I Am And What I Am Not
Valid Vicky

I am cheerful happiness, not life of stress.
I am contentment, not living with resentment.
I am happy to see you, not what do I need from you.
I am chillin' in peace, not running from police.
I've got kids to feed, not buying your weed.
I am early nights, not shoutin' and fights.
And one thing that's clear, that now you're not here;
I'm finally free to do the best for me.

My Life, My Rules
Anon

I still think about the night when waiting for the noise to stop.
The pain fades and I'm still here.
I would ask myself if I can go on.
Can I take hold of the fear, grip it tight and run with it?
When I lost control, I found anger.
The anger found me
I loosened my grip
on all the creature comforts
in order to pursue sanity.
My mind was black with rage and I knew
only I could take responsibility for myself
and how my life would turn out.
I tried to keep moving
it was hard as fuck,
but by prioritising my recovery
I left the haters in the dust.
Goodbye.
My grief meant I wouldn't waste another day,
I wouldn't give up on myself and I would choose life.
My life, my rules.
I don't know if anyone noticed but
I felt like I had died and came back to life.
You were all left behind and focused on the old me,
meanwhile I grew wings and flew.
Look at me I'm flying.

It took all of my being you know,
to avoid your traps and savagery.
You underestimated me that time but
I know you won't rush to do that again.
Counting sheep while I ease into my restful sleep.
My bed, my home, my haven can't be corrupted
by germs don't you know.
Don't count me out.
Tomorrow is my day, tomorrow and every day is mine and
you're fucked if you try and take it away.

Never Again
Fabulously Fearless

I treated you kindly,
I showered you with love and gifts.
In return you gave me heartache,
Misery and pain.
I see you now for what you really are,
A sad, pathetic, selfish cunt.
Someone who didn't deserve the kindness,
The trust and love I gave you with my whole being.
God blessed you with four of the most beautiful bundles of joy
you treated them like dirt.
Your jealousy and control is now abundantly clear.
My freedom eyes and warrior spirit ensure
that you will NEVER be able to inflict
your bullying and hateful behaviour on us again.

Processing Emotions
Anon

Sadness and grief: I watched my world getting smaller before my eyes. A free spirit with no rules, I had to meet his requirements and live behind his walls. Powerlessness consumed me. I could not speak, I felt like a victim, like a child. I fought the pain to push it down and resist the harshness of reality, but it did not work. Fooling my friends and my family was light work, but fooling myself nearly broke my back.

Anger: Someone I loved and trusted used me as a dump. I am that rage filled emotional dustbin that only knows how to strike inwards. Anger was ok for others, I buffered it like a soundproof wall, but I looked around to be heard when it was my turn to hurt and was met with indifference, so I knew somehow I'd not yet earned the right.

Peace and acceptance: The only way I got peace was by hitting bedrock and working my way back. Some things I'll never accept but I choose to live; sad truths are a heavy burden but won't stop me from growing. I'm on a path and pick flowers on the way to brighten my day; the ones I love I learn to hold loosely.

Survivors And Thrivers

Anon

What it means to be a woman:

Giving birth to the next generation of soldiers. Breaking the chains of the past. Owning my shit. Taking responsibility. Being alive. Truly living even when it hurts.
The best thing about being a woman:
Our magical bodies that create and inspire art and life.
The hardest thing about being a woman:
My body is not my own, I'm public property. I'm not seen as human.
Be tough and be your own best friend. Love yourself the way you are,
Practice happiness and fuck being kind.

That's Feminism

Anon

Fight for females, that's feminism, fuck being kind.
Exclusively for liberating women,
Men are not invited, that's your shit to examine.
Inspired women drew boundaries and battled for us
Night and day, we fight on for justice.
It's for our daughters, sisters and mothers that we will never give up.
Strangle the fate our body gave us and
Melt the threat with your heart sisters.

HAPPY

WOMEN'S DAY

THERE IS NO LIMIT TO

WHAT WE, AS WOMEN, CAN

ACCOMPLISH.

MICHELLE OBAMA

March

Sisters
Outstanding Obi

Starved, desperate for change.
Inundated and perplexed.
Survivors we are.
Together we emerge,
Each one from her shell.
Reborn related,
Sisters in arms, victors we are.

S.I.S.T.E.R.S.
Valid Vicky

Someone who knows you to the core,
Instinct links you ever more.
Supporting, laughing, sharing deep,
Truth and secrets both to keep.
Everlasting love.
Relentlessly caring.
Stronger together.

Being A Woman
Fabulously Fearless

Being a woman means I am a little bit girl,
A little bit old woman,
And a bit somewhere in between.

I have crawled through barbed wire
And swam through warm currents.
I have climbed mountains to get here.

I have walked over hot coals,
I ran in the rain,
I have encountered blisters and sorrow,
Bear hugs and bliss.

I have run from monsters,

Those that were real and those in mind,
To find my calm.

I have overcome the obstacle course of life,
Sometimes it was easy,
Sometimes it was a fucking hard graft.

I had many friends,
And just as many foes,
But throughout it all,
One truth remained,
I was here all along.

Being a woman means
I am fucking amazing.

Sisters
Fabulously Fearless

Sisterly love is the best love.
I love my sister, and she loves me.
So much love between my sister and I.
Together forever, you and I.
Even when we're old and grey.
Remember me, as I will you.
Sisterly love is the best love in the world.

Womanhood
Fabulously Fearless Fee

Wise warrior.
Old before her time.
Magnificent.
And
Nurturing all of the time.
Happiness she waives, for those she loves.
Over and over again even though she knows.
Over and over she will be hurt.
Duty-bound, womanhood lives on.

What It Means To Be A Woman
Lovely Lucy

Being a woman means glory and pride,
That may be a surprise,
But to your demise we always rise,
Rise like a sunrise.

I have crawled through dark tunnels and grime,
Overshadowed by your lies.
Torture and bitterness tried to make me wild,
But to my surprise it never overrides.
You display your projection
what really lies deep within
your soul taken by The devil.

I have walked over eggshells,
Dying inside not to say a word as you would hail.
You spoke in so much detail, full of arrogant pride,
Describing your combats of battle with what you call degenerates,
But we both really know that's all from your low self-esteem,
Shame and non-existent validation.

I have run from pain and fear,
No more I hear.
I am enough.
I am love.
I am facing you with my bluff,
I will succeed no matter what.
I am enough.

I have overcome shame and guilt.
Loss and abandonment.
I am protected,
My root is on fire,
No more I hear.
I am free with power and glory,
And your name is not in my vocabulary.
Being a woman means,
A journey of moments put together
like a sea of embedded emotions.

You ride low, high and flow in full alignment
knowing what had happened was
your lesson or reason.

Right now is a gift and your future is
an excitement of delight and honour,
Welcome it with full conviction.
I wouldn't change being a woman,
I love the free flow of my ocean,
Deep, wild and natural.

I am that dope potion,
Full of imagination.
I can guide your energy to unlimited expectations.
When you experience this orgasmic explosion,
You will want to celebrate us women for our healing,
Guiding you to this floatation of relaxation.

Freedom
Amazing Asha

Freedom is so priceless.
So is time, and it's all borrowed.
So when you're sad and cry, just know,
It'll be better tomorrow.
But tomorrow isn't promised so I'll start today,
To reclaim my freedom
So I won't sway.
Standing strong I'll let the rain
wash away the pain that felt so foreign to me.
Scars heal and so will I!
I love my freedom and I finally know why.

Freedom Poem
Jazzy Jane

13 December 2022
19:32
Staring at my phone, I'm feeling very alone, but I'm safe and free,

building a new home just for me.
We started as friends, caring gestures, a little DIY, in exchange for a natter,
your victimised stories made me feel sorry for you,
who knew that multiple times I would feel so discarded and used?

Your women had been crazy, act 3 scene 1,
I listened lazily, little did I know, I would star in your sadistic show.
We'd walk the dog far, and then camp under the stars,
each Christmas Eve an inch closer, on the sofa.
One day I was broken, it caught me off guard,
you kissed me at tea time and it opened my heart.

A rollercoaster started, not long had we departed, the highs were
dissolving.
Your lies and addiction turned to threats and gaslighting.
So then you left, said your love was too strong,
too cowardly to face this great union that was going so wrong.

For months I was bereft.
The cycle started again, this time I knew it was doomed,
you weren't the innocent neighbour that popped up with a spoon.
My actions were being tracked, my car you sourced was scrapped,
the breakfast date part three left me phoneless and attacked.

So my reaction caught attention, fuelled your need to lie to everyone,
you cleverly played the hero, looking after sick auntie?
Doting dad to authorities, manipulated my own family and still love
bombing me.
I've never left someone running, in fear for my life, from neighbours to
lovers,
stealing moments under the covers.
When homelessness struck I kept running,
read books, and with new freedom eyes I know that wasn't love.

Freedom
Camouflage Claire

Freedom is a word; a George Michael song; a state of being; a state
of mind... what you lose when told you're wrong.

WORDS FROM WARRIOR WOMEN

Freedom is a right when violence is left.
When tables turn and
nightmares burn leaving ashes made from shite.

Freedom is what freedom does and
believing that's the key.
The jailor's gone and I've moved on...
Freedom is me.

My Freedom Eyes
Valid Vicky

I see you for what you are,
I see you don't want to be a better person,
To treat people well.
I see you feel you're entitled,
Well I'm entitled as well.
Entitled to my life back,
Free to be happy,

Positive me.
No longer will you undermine the roots

Of this beautiful tree.
I don't want you anymore,
The love I had has gone.
Now I feel pity,

You were once somebody's son.
I have realised so many things,
All of them key,
Now I choose to spend my time
With those who share values with me.
I feel a strange contentment
Where for years I've felt alone,
'Cos deep inside I now respect myself,
I'm stronger and I've grown.
You don't know where I am.
I feel safe.
I feel secure.

In fact I feel like I'm on holiday,
behind MY OWN front door.

I know I will still hear from you...
And in moments of weakness
I consider it for a split second.
Then I remember the list I wrote of "that time."
Such a powerful list to remind me;
Remember that time he did this,
That time he did that.
I'm never going back to you,
You're just a fucking twat.

Freedom
Fabulously Fearless

I look deep within my domain,
Only a soul is found,
But this soul is me free from a man's poverty towards me.
Freedom is a wealth that we craved,
Only those of us who have been chained
Understand what it is to be truly free.

I Am
Valid Vicky

I am walking.
My head is filled with insecurities but I am walking.
I am walking away,
The fear of what might happen or what you might do is still there.
My heart beats hard.
I am unsure of where I am going.
I am walking in silence because I have left the noise behind.
The noise that until now has surrounded me, inescapable.
I am not where I need to be yet.
But I am walking.
More purposely than before.

Slowly I see that my surroundings are changing.

The noise is behind me,
I hear silence.
And then I hear something that breaks my silence.
I stop dead in my tracks and listen.
It is the sound of a bird singing,
It is familiar like I heard it before,
But it hasn't been there for a while.
I listen to the birdsong and I can hear more.
I hear the babbling of the stream
The sound of summer breezes in the trees,
Like a switch has been flicked in my brain.

Has the chaos of my life 'til now blocked my ability to hear?
To sense what is real?
Or did the birds stop their song
Because of the darkness that engulfed me.
I do not have an answer but now I am walking
And I am feeling more sure of my direction.
I am walking in the direction I have chosen.
I am listening to what my ears were meant to hear.
I am further away from my noise,
But know the noise might return.
I am not going to stop walking,
And now I can sense what is real
I will not let this disappear again.

Today
Fabulously Fearless

Today she took on a battle and won,
Today she showed her true warrior spirit,
Today she came,
She overcame and she conquered all the demons of the past,
The system and those who tried to break her.
Today, my friends, is a day to thank the Lord for miracles, each and every
one.

Today; I am stronger because you lifted me when I was weak,
I am braver because you held me when I was afraid,
I am a fighter because you taught me how to get back up when I was down,

I am bold and beautiful because you believed in me when I did not believe in myself,
I am free because you loved me just for being me.

Time Is A Healer
Fabulously Fearless

Time is a healer, of that I am finally sure,
It simply takes time to get there.
I have often believed that I had been destroyed or buried alive
but now I know like a seed, I had just been planted.
It's been hard to push through and start growing again,
but no longer a fragile sapling;
like an old oak I am once again mighty and strong.
I've been hoping for a miracle, some sign
that it's all worthwhile and I have not been disappointed.
Yesterday, that miracle was long awaited,
today ask me how many I've been sent?
They are so many, I lost count.
Tomorrow is never promised so I live for the
gift of the present which is today.
Today I am healing and blessed.

I am grateful for all my blessings, big and small.
I am worthy of all the love and joy in the world.
I am strong enough to live, survive and
thrive without you and despite you.
I am getting closer to being truly happy in my own skin.
I am an amazing, kind, fearless, fabulous
and ferociously independent, sassy woman.
I will continue standing in and speaking my truth.
I am going to continue to be amazing in every possible way.

I Am
Lovely Lucy

I am present,
Present in this glorious moment.
I am here,

Yet I am gone.
I am sitting in this air,
Yet this air is sometimes suffocating to my very core.
I am free yet still a prisoner to this fuckery.
I am happy yet sad at the loss of my dignity.

I am that escapist who likes to walk in a deep forest,
Looking at other aspects of life,
wondering if they feel what we feel,
Or am I just too much?
Sometimes that's why they leave me free.

I am love,
Love that walks and beats,
Radiating a talent of heat.
Not that shallow type who pretends,
But really they are a love of cheat,
But you know energy never lies,
As it never dies.

I am observant to that grime,
That grime that leaks out of your fucking mouth,
That salivating salivator that spits out your lies.
I am aware and I'll never believe,
I am strong yet feel weak.
You may see me as this light,
But yet I come with dark as everything is duality.

I am still yet growing,
On this journey called life.
Some need to back the hell up,
I have found my voice,
My throat chakra is open,
Raring to speak.

I am calm,
I am peace,
But most of all,
I am grateful to be still here
Speaking my truth,
As lies don't run that deep.

Superhero
Notable Naomi

I am me.
For years I tried to change.
I tried to be the person that my perpetrator
And others expected of me.
This wasn't happening.
It was like being told to learn to forgive,
Yet when I forgave
I felt more was being thrown my way.
I kept giving.
It wasn't working.

It was a reminder that I should try harder,
Do better,
Be the amazing person I should be.
Hold down a job.
Look after my family.
Bring in a wage.
Look beautiful.
Wear a mask.
Wear the fashion expected of me.
Speak when spoken to.
Don't say too much.

In all of this I wanted to be accepted as me.
In accepting me as myself,
I now know it is the only way to move forward.

So going back to superheroes it had to be me.
No way practically perfect in any way, but me.
I am proud to be me.

This doesn't say in any way that it hasn't been hard.
I'm learning with trauma, it has to be revisited
In order to keep on moving forward.
I have to keep working on it.

I have called myself Captain Survivor.
I have survived.

I am moving on.
I am learning to be kind to myself.

So, Captain Survivor.
I am fine as myself.
No excuses made.

However, in my picture who knows what's under the coat,
Those slight flashes of colour that seep through.
The change that can be made and is now allowed to happen.
A wonderful charity called WE:ARE has supported me in my journey.
They continue to support as they know that trauma can last a lifetime.
They do such amazing work.
I don't know where I would be without their support.

No Naming No Shaming
Outstanding Obi

The code I lived by the code I was to die by
Back against the wall legs swinging in air
Arms akimbo breathless cause my airways was blocked
No naming no shaming
No telling of how I became an expert in masking
Black Eyed, tear-stained face, broken ribs and yes a broken heart
An actor playing the happy partner
Broken, bruised, famished, naked and alone
No naming no shaming
A walk in the park, a meeting at church, waiting for the bus
From my bloodshot eyes veiled by my shades I see
The all too familiar markings on Jane by my right
And on Eve by my left!
If we are this much where are the men I wonder
Bonding in the park a pact we form
Karma is we succeeding
Survivors triumphing!!!

I Am Alive
Anon

I am out of control,
I am blind rage and confusion,
With lost self and negligible pity.

I am shock,
I am horror,
I am disbelief and deceased.
It hurts your eyes to see me,
But simultaneously you feast.

I am biscuits,
Box sets and my trusty dressing gown
Who still comforts me to this day.
I am slow and steady,
And I am shit scared to move
Lest I fuck it up again.

I am weak,
I am worthless.
I am crazy and reckless,
I feel like you enjoy this.

I am in need of intervention,
You appoint yourself my saviour.
I am deserving of smears and lies,
I am your demon in the mirror.

I am alone.
I am still slow and steady,
But not scared to move this time.
I am medicated,
I am medicated,
I'm driving and I can't see straight...
I am withdrawing.

Am I alive?
I am alive.

Shocking as it feels I can be found
With my feet on solid ground;
I pinch myself.
I am in control,
I choose life and I choose freedom;
It's my biggest fear to lose it,
But if there's doubts I refuse to hear them.

Endings
Sensual Sarah

There is beauty in endings
My love is blue singing the blues
what to do, when lovers tear each other apart
Sad News
Broken Pieces shattered dreams once shared
Love on the run
A Bleeding heart
Like a dart to the chest
From love to detest
When it's love we don't snuff our lover's joy out
Stolen your heart to steal your joy
For what Boy? A sick game of love and pain
Ripped my heart out put my sanity to the test
I must Protest, I don't accept this fuckery as love.
it's agony, you're killing me
I have been dying for crumbs of your Love.

No Regrets
Sensual Sarah

I often wonder why?
then tell myself, No regrets
Dry my eye, eyes streaming
Brush my shoulder off
I've hit rock bottom
Broken to pieces
lost the light in my eyes
dull and dead inside

the only thing worse than death is being
destroyed by the one you love
Toxic Lovers a deadly losing game
won't leave you the same
there's light after toxic Love, get out.

Mind
Sensual Sarah

I mind my business
I mind My thoughts
Thought I loved you
Thought you loved me
Thought wrong
it never had an ending until now
goodbye toxic lover.
thought you had my back
thought our love was rare
false twin

Thoughts of Without You
Sensual Sarah

Without you, I am me again
Without you, the fire that fuels me would go out, I am hooked

Without you, my heart can rest
Without you, I can sleep easy
Without you, I can breathe again
Without you, Peace can fill me up
Without you, the feeling of dread will leave

Without you, I must be
Without you, no you and me
Without You, I can thrive, living a life fully alive
Without You, I will love who I am again

Without you, my path won't be egg shells wherever I step
Without you, I breath easy deep loving breaths

Without you, my heart can heal and open to love
Without Regret.

And The Sun Shone Down
Notable Naomi

The night sky lifted.
Bright blue crept in.
Marshmallow clouds scattered throughout.
The sun shining down.

Glorifying the flowers just blooming into June.
Shedding a beautiful haze onto the view.
Amazing.
Wonderful.
New growth and Summer are maybe here.

Love Mess
Sensual Sarah

Caught off guard when all my walls were down
in love defenceless.

Sisterhood
Sensual Sarah

Can't keep us apart, tried to isolate us
Hear the Cries of Fearless Women's Hearts
Soul Sisters united in pain walking together into bright tomorrows

Scrap Heap
Sensual Sarah

Riding the Love wave
Ghost Train full of discarded lovers
Disfigured hearts

Broken and bruised
ripped out
A Scrap Heap of hearts

I am the One
Sensual Sarah

I am the one
Rolled into one
I am the One
A Queen
Lone Wolf
a Longing
Not Belonging

Know Thyself
Sensual Sarah

I am becoming
I am Joyous
I am wisdom
I am Beauty
I am strength
I am my vulnerabilities
I am Peace
I am driven
I am divine
I am all knowing and I am
I know nothing simultaneously
I am Self Love
the only true wisdom is
knowing you know nothing

Dear Wise Warrior Women
Sensual Sarah

I belong here
You Belong Here

we Belong here

I am my lover and best friend
serene moments
maddening actions
a reckless streak
born wild and free
a pure-hearted girl
wear my heart on my sleeve
You put up with so much
it's been hell
Baby girl, Hell Fires got nothing
on the pit of your stomach
Never Put a Good Woman Down
Never Keep a Good Woman Down

Me, Myself, I
Sensual Sarah

Mother of all comebacks
Agony to Ecstasy
Misery entirely, Red flags ignored

Youth Has no age when you're dying inside

Stopped accepting toxic love
I am every Woman
Love is my birth right
Fighting for tomorrow

I can love myself better
Moments lost to time
Exited That Story
a painful blur, survival mode no more

Misery of his making became me
Young in love and trauma bonded
Stuck in a rut loving you
Exit plan needed
Love shouldn't cost my sanity and dignity

Fuck toxic love, broken bones and promises

If this is how You Love. No thanks

Break the Chains
Sensual Sarah

Break the Chains
In seclusion, no illusion
Just delusion, my confusion
Dead Romance

Fill her head with your lies
she is no longer Eating your
Bullshit for breakfast
Lies and excuses for dinner
Crumbs of your love, effort and time
An absent you for Pudding
you're Kidding.
Dead Love on a Plate.

I Am A Broken Chain
Sensual Sarah

I am beautiful
I am strength
I am soft and gentle
I am fierce
I am love
I am divine
I am my own best friend
I am peace
I am Joyous
I am Wisdom
I am Clarity
I am wiser
I am healing
I am lessons learned

I am Breaking The Chain
We Are Broken Chains
Together we Rise.

Peace Not Pieces
Sensual Sarah

Oooh, didn't cha know
I am my own best friend
wasn't always friendly
didn't always treat her with Love
A dove sent from the Heavens
to fill my heart with Peace
Peace not Pieces

In Lust We Trust
Sensual Sarah

I don't trust myself
not to do wrong
not to stay open to hurt myself
I got hurt on purpose but by accident just to feel the pain
Now it wont quit hurting
But I quit
I don't mean wrong by you
I do wrong by me, just look and see
the Mess that is me
I don't even remember the She I used to Be
Like a butterfly I want to transform. Be New Again

The Edge
Sensual Sarah

I want to go to the edge of the Earth
I want to Kiss its peaks
the edge of my heart
when I see paradise I know I will want to keep living
and carry its beauty with me always

I am Basalheath
I am Birmingham
I am Kings Norton
I am Kings Heath and Stirchley
I am where I walk and where I have walked
I am the women that trod this path before me, guiding the way
I am worthy and I am worth all of my footsteps
Let me Keep Walking
thank you for walking beside me

To Have Hope
Sassy Survivor

To have hope means never to let go of your dreams,
That everything will turn out alright in the end.
The childlike naïveté that keeps optimism alive.
Hoping for a better future is what kept me alive for so long,
This need for a happily ever after saved me from destruction.
Hope looks like a candle in my heart,
A crocus poking through the February snow,
The smiles on my children's faces,
The look of my soulmate as our gaze connects.
Hope sounds like tinkling streams, baby giggles, and 'I love yous.'
Having hope is a risk that is crucial to your survival,
Hope conflicts with depression.
My hope keeps me alive,
It has often been the only thing that has done,
The eternal anticipation that life must get better.
To instil hope is to become someone's knight in shining armour.
Give a person hope and you can help someone to save themselves,
The weapon that they need to conquer the demons.
Here is a short list of things that I hope for;
Total freedom from the dominator,
Healing from my trauma,
Reconciliation with lost family,
To dance in warm rain with my soulmate,
For my children to grow into happy contented adults,
To be financially secure,
That my happy ever after lasts forever.
That the people I love know how much I love them.

That the truth will set me free.
My hopes feel achievable.
That's the thing with hope,
While you hold onto it the impossible is possible,
The improbable is achievable.
Hope springs eternal.
Hope can save your life.

Write Your New Story
Lily

When hope is gone it feels like you're drowning,
When you are constantly at breaking point,
Coping with more than is possible
And life still keeps throwing things at you.
When you no longer have the energy to cope
With everything that life is demanding of you.
How can you trust that you have the power to survive?
When the one person who is supposed to love you the most in the world
Is the one that makes you cry.
Know that they are not the one.
Love does not work like that.
That is not love, that is abuse.
When all you want is to resign from humanity,
To hibernate away from expectation and demand,
Look towards the light.
Know that there is only one life,
Grab it and make the most of it.
Even a little thing can change your life,
What may seem like an insignificant positive can change your future.
Take the seed that hope plants within you,
Cultivate it, nurture it,
And grow into your own person.
Turn the page,
Write your new story.

Hope
Lovely Lucy

To have hope means
To believe in what you already have.
Just look deeper within,
You will live not just as a dreamer but as a believer.
Hoping for a better future as I sit here waiting to discover,
The mysteries I uncover.
Hope looks like a sweet whisper,
Sparks the heat and makes you deliver.
Hope sounds like that flowing river, wavy, unearthly,
But always in a constant direction.
Having hope is a risk that you
may fall down as you climb up.
Each step,
You grow taller.
My hope keeps me sane,
Motivated and safe throughout,
So I will shine like that sun beaming down.
To instil hope is to take action.
Keep moving,
You are growing,
Here is a short list of things I hope for;
Gratitude,
Patience,
A retreat in a garden of pure bliss,
Swaying branches of deep brown roots,
Tilting back and forth,
Delighting in the heat.
My hopes feel real,
They are here ready for me to experience,
Dance with them under the moon, light, sun.
The hope that never dies as it always begins.
When hope is gone,
It's all in your mind,
Don't despair,
It's just a cycle of your page in your chapter,
You always know the answer,
Your energy never lies.
You have the power to rise above any obstacle,

All the answers lie within,
Just quiet the mind,
Wait to listen to your great intuition.
Hope is like a dark winter's night,
Long and dreary,
But then comes the morning light.
You watch all that change with trust and humanity,
Knowing your future is you,
Being just you,
I am hope like that seed in the dark,
Growing into the light,
No race,
No acts,
Just now I can see through my sight,
Believe me, it is shining bright.

Courage
Lovely Lucy

Staring through the crimson rose glass,
I see my worth staring back at me.
Fierce and strong just like the warrior I am,
I was tore but not no more,
I connected to my shadow self,
Embraced all parts of me,
The good, the bad and ugly.

I laugh in the face of defeat.
Defeat of what?
A journey which has led me here.
I listened to my intuition,
Intuition of knowing one self.
Being connected to trust and protection,
Yes that dances like a swirl inside me,
Contrasting my energy to free flow to every cell,
Giving life and breath to my extraordinary self,
I am here, in the now,
I live through each moment,
I trust, I love,
I am enough.

Hope
Lovely Lyndsey

Hope is all that's left.

Within my darkest days, Isolation was my closest friend,
Losing relationships, family and friends thinking it's the end,
The addiction made me want to leave and escape all my pain,
I took a hard look at my life, and hope is all I have left to gain.

I am worth more than you all think,
My past is history, and my present is just a kink,
A kink in this chapter, that will pass.

They say that winding roads lead to great destinations,
But I feel so far from home, from where I should be,

Hope is my only key!

All I hear is my heartbeat thudding through my chest,
It's so hard to hold back the tears, and look my best.
But inside, I am breaking down, I am losing my patience!
I'm so far from home, so far from who I was!
Now I'm scared of the dark!

Please, higher powers, I need you to bring me home,

Give me strength, give me HOPE.

Hope Reigns
Hopeful Holly

Hope is like a glimmer
In a vast dark sky,
It weaves and wanders
But it is yours
It is mine,

It may seem to flicker,
To threaten to snuff;
But I assure you

It is more than enough!

For its glow lights the way,
Its warmth shall soothe,
And its faint flicker
Is but a clever dance
That threads its way
Through debris and carnage...
Oh yes,
It knows the way!

And smiling triumphantly,
It will declare a brand new day
Where joy can nestle
So that love can say;
I will never surrender!
I will not give up!
I will conquer these troubles,
I shall overcome!

When hope reigns
We shall cast out shadows
Of darting disarmed soldiers,
Shamed into the light of night!
And our weapons?
Glorious measures
Of faith and trust,
In me,
And in you,
And at last
we shall be forever
Just as we were always
Meant to be!

Safe At Last
Outstanding Obi

Four sons and a daughter.
Everything I'll need,
Yes I got the best of you!

My seeds, my reward from this anguish,
Incredible but true.
Never again would my best be found in you.
I won the war you began.
Safe at last, my seeds and I
Miles away from you,
Empty of us!

Decorating My Future
Anon

I want a beautifully decorated flat.
I want to start by painting my bathroom.
I've chosen a pale green to make me feel
light and airy when I enter in the morning.
I want to put my personality into the walls.
I want to make the most of even having
the choice to do so after renting for years.
I want to challenge my DIY skills and
grow my confidence in a new ability.
Achieving this will move me forward in my goals.
I will be happy to tick it off the list (I love lists).
I will have a reminder everyday of my choice,
My space,
My potential. I'll feel unstoppable,
I'll feel ready for the next challenge,
Powerful and in control of my life and destiny

Picnic
Fabulously Fearless

I'm going on a picnic,
my friend's will all be there.
I'm going on a picnic and
there won't be any drama, bullshit or hard stares.
I'm going on a picnic and
I'm going to eat, laugh, and be merry.
I'm going on a picnic,
It will the best one ever,
'Cos thank fuck you won't be there!

WORDS FROM **WARRIOR WOMEN**

You Don't Need That Anymore
Valid Vicky

You will realise that you don't need those eyes,
The beautiful brown ones that once lit you up inside.
Now every look at you diminishes your pride,
For they are a disguise.

You will realise that you don't need those lips,
Once love's kiss, passion and bliss,
Turned into something amiss.
Spitting lines at you,
You don't deserve this.

You don't need those hands,
At first strong and secure,
They are your prison,
The lock on the door.

You don't need that any more.

Four Words
Anon

Shame – quiet shame, because I don't want you to know I feel it. Head high and proud but burning on the inside. If I ignore the comments will they stop? Yes they do, but the pain does not.

Greed – with all the luck and benefits of body I have been afforded, I still want more and more. I could spend the earth but still have a shopping list spilling down my pad.

Chance – by chance I have this body that functions and views pretty nice, just through luck not from being good or honest. He gave it and can take it but I'll stay rooted while my strength allows.

Hair – the source of pride and shame, of strength that I claim. Grow this, cut that, thread here and laser there but remember it's a secret you can't share.

Freedom And Empowerment
Notable Naomi

The daisies intertwined, weaving their way in and out reaching for the sky.
Each individual stalk takes a different path to achieve their goal.
To reach out and bloom.
Some having added assistance on the way to produce colour, bright and beautiful.
Some dulled with life and not expressing their true worth and brilliance, being held back.
Each having their own journey at times so hard they couldn't see the sun, or light.
Just a glimmer was all that was needed.
A drop of rain to encourage change and growth.

Finding The Light
Notable Naomi

I unearthed a small chunk of earth that had taken the light and joy out of my life for far too long.
A small glimmer appeared and through that tiny gap appeared the sun, the blue sky, the clouds and bird song.
A Light I hadn't seen before.
An acceptance, and maybe an understanding of myself.
For too long, I have been buried in the depths of my pain, past, and unforgiving memories.
The small chink of light gave me a chance to escape the tortures of my mind, of a life I no longer live,
To open my heart to the warmth that might actually reach me in times where I haven't completely shut my heart down.
Does this give me licence to change? To be me, to be free and uncaring of the taunts that trouble my mind?
Oh wouldn't it be amazing if it did!

A change where I didn't feel so defensive of the effort I put into my day.
To be able to breathe the fresh air, to inhale the life that I feel has been taken from me for far too long and to live,
To dance in my dreams and sing as loud as I please with whatever words that come into my mind, and not care one little bit what others may think.
To be accepting and maybe one day to love me, myself.

Wouldn't that be amazing!

Maybe one day as each chunk of earth is thrown out and dismissed, I may have a clearer picture ahead of me,
But for now I will bask in the chink of light that warms my very soul and hope for a brighter happier future.
The tears came, they flooded out of my parched dry loveless body.
They rolled down my cheeks and spilled out from the centre of my being.
From the depths of my pain I unearthed memories deeply buried as they were too hard to absorb at the time.
I breathed deeply as I took the time to know that part of me that had been hidden away.
I expelled the history and pain in those few hours, my body and soul let me be free.

I had a small space to create, to find the words to write as my thoughts reminded me that I could now strive to be free.
I gave myself time to heal, and needed rest in my soul and decided that now was the time to be me.
Who is me?
I have no idea, but I will one day find the person I was meant to be.

I Grew You In My Garden
Anon

"I grew you in my garden",
He said,
"I will give you everything that you need,
You are my most precious possession,
My perfect little seed."

"It is I who will water you, with cool cold fresh spring water.
It is I who will turn your lavish leaves to the sunlight,
My precious little daughter
But why are you wilting?
I have given you everything that you need
You are just like your brother,
I have raised another weed."

I grew in your garden

I grew in your garden,
Thank you for the light.
See, not all plants need so much water,
What you think I need is not always right.
I did try to tell you, I did try to say—
"If you keep watering me like that, I'll wilt away one day.".
Though my soil is saturated, and I find it hard to breathe,
My brother is a sunflower, a very special seed
He told me when I was growing, to look deep inside my leaves
For everything I am, is all I'll ever need

Poppy Field
Real Rachel

When we met I stepped out into a poppy field,
Red flags stretched as far as my eyes would see,
I welcomed every single red flag into my home.
Flowers on the table,
My cards were laid out for you to take your pick.
Turns out you were a prick.
Shit.

I look at you,
Looking at me,
You won't know
How much I love you
Until you have your own.

That's a mother's love.
You better get well soon.
I love you baby.
Now please go back to sleep,
Because your mum needs a break.

How the fuck can a man
Think he is superior to a woman,
When a woman grew him from seed
With her own body;
And he is only here today
Because of a woman.

And yet still he thinks it's a man's world.
What the fuck?

Thank you.
I got caught in a storm today.
Hail, rain, thunder.
I ran home as the sky lit up around me.
I laughed, splashing through the puddles,
Drenched to the bone.
I beamed,
Looking down at my babe all cosy under the plastics.
My makeup ran down my face,
My straightened hair curled,
My trainers soaked through,
The thunder rumbled through the floor,
Cars splashed puddles all over me.
I ran,
And ran,
And laughed,
And smiled;
Because no matter how bad the storm gets,
It is nothing compared to what you put me through.
Nothing.
So thank you for giving me this strength
I never knew I had inside,
For this baby,
And this new love,
For the stormiest of days.
Thank you.

On your high horse you trotted in,
My hero in tin foil armour.
Twinkling,
Crinkling,
You weren't my hero.
Heroin.
Hero in.
Another reality,
Your fantasy,
Red flags...
The poppy field only drew me further in.

Warnings ignored with that first hit.
I surrendered.
Absolutely fucking hooked.

Breakdown To Break Through
Lovely Laura

Sometimes you have to travel alone. Stop. Pause.
Be with yourself, before you become overthrown
By things you crave, the reasons unknown.

I fly blind, it's all I can do.
After the life I was living, so untrue.
My thoughts are fraught but I'm trying my best,
To keep them caught and understand what is making me this distraught.

Sometimes I get lost, derailed by my own depression.
What a mess I've been left in.
What's happened to me?
Where am I?
Will I be like this forever?

I tried to hold on, my mental health hanging by a thread,
But you came back only to push me over the edge,
And, sure I felt dead.

Pain held a mirror to my own attachment trauma.
Created by my own father,
Something up until now I've kept behind an armour.

THANK YOU FOR BUSTING ME OPEN

This was a new kind of shit.
I thought I had my fair share of horror in life,
This time I quit.

Something really broke inside,
I'm tired of hiding it.

I discovered me through cruelty.

In a way I'm glad I snapped under the brutality,
Enough is enough now.
I'm happy to be alone and free, having therapy.

I thought that I could keep it together,
But this time I'm really changed forever.
Life has crushed me into what I was destined to be.
But my inner child is now dying to be seen,
And I'm coming clean to everyone,
He won this time;
But fuck it,
I win for me.

In The Darkness
Strong Sammie

Sometimes in the darkness we remember the walls closing in,
We remember the nights of horror,
The days of torment,
All from someone we thought of as kin.
Remembering the hot breath on your neck,
That cold touch of pain,
Nothing in return but a peck.
It's okay to remember,
But what we need to remember now is,
We can turn the light on!

Growing Out Of The Dark
Amazing Anna

If you ask about my struggle
I would say put a mirror in front of you and see true me
The trapped body of me
You might wonder
What makes me strong today
That's my own true self
As I grow into a beautiful woman
I found myself in an oasis
In my dream I was standing somewhere

I could see the real me
It's dark sometimes
But there's always a real brightness
And that holds me back from being
trapped inside my dark world
I can see a huge hollow of
emptiness within my other self
I could feel that and release it
To surround myself with hope and courage.

Time To Be Me
Notable Naomi

Finding the light
I unearthed a small chunk of earth that had taken the light and joy out of my life for far too long. A small glimmer appeared and through that tiny gap appeared the sun, the blue sky, the clouds and bird song. A Light I hadn't seen before. An acceptance and maybe an understanding of myself. For too long I have been buried in the depths of my pain, past and unforgiving memories.
The small chink of light gave me a chance to escape the tortures of my mind of a life I no longer live. To open my heart to the warmth that might actually reach me in times where I haven't completely shut my heart down. Does this give me licence to change? to be me, to be free and uncaring of the taunts that trouble my mind.
Oh wouldn't it be amazing if it did.
A change where I didn't feel so defensive of the effort I put into my day.
To be able to breathe the fresh air, to inhale the life that I feel has been taken from me for far too long and to live, to dance in my dreams and sing as loud as I please with whatever words that come into my mind and not care one little bit what others may think.
To be accepting and maybe one day to love me, myself . Wouldn't that be amazing!
Maybe one day as each chunk of earth is thrown out and dismissed I may have a clearer picture ahead of me, but for now I will bask in the chink of light that warms my very soul and hope for a brighter happier future.
The tears came, they flooded out of my parched dry loveless body.
They rolled down my cheeks and spilled out from the centre of my being.
From the depths of my pain I unearthed memories deeply buried as they were too hard to absorb at the time.

I breathed deeply as I took the time to know that part of me that had been hidden away.
I expelled the history and pain in those few hours that my body and soul let me be free.
I had a small space to create to find the words to write down as my thoughts reminded me that I could now strive to be free.
I gave myself time to heal and much-needed rest in my soul and decided that now was the time to be me.
Who is me.
I have no idea, but I will one day find the person I was meant to be.

Different Seasons
Notable Naomi

I went to bed last night and my mind wouldn't sleep.
I need to draw, but also get something written down.
I couldn't stop thinking about a bulb buried in the soil,
no sign of growth, but keeping warm under the cold earth waiting for that moment,
Maybe in Spring when it would start to emerge.
The earth I looked at as my life, or indeed anyone's life.
All having a different story under the ground nestling the bulb.
I looked at getting to know someone, the true person inside the mask maybe.
Needing to get through that soil,
The makeup of life to be able to emerge and maybe one day to bloom.
I look at my life in different seasons with this in mind.
The difficult times when you hide away,
Find anything comforting to get you through the day.
This is the winter.
I look at a person in the street.
glamorous young lady, high heels, smile on her face.
The look of confidence, although this is just the outer shell, the flower.
None of us know what the other carries on a daily basis,
The hurt inside someone's heart, the inner struggles.
What's beneath the soil or indeed in it.
A touch of kindness, a gentle nurturing word and the bulb starts to move,
The little green shoot springing forth into the daylight absorbing the sun.
This is the spring!
Reaching out wanting to grow, wanting to bloom, but not quite there.

All the time beneath the surface lies the soil made up with its life story.
The bulb needs just the right environment to grow as we do as humans.
Sometimes it takes longer for one to bloom, as it does in life,
And we get knocked back into our bulb-like state wondering
whether next spring will be our time to grow;
To escape and spread any kind of beauty that may spill out of our petals.
The summer is just around the corner and like life
we have no idea how this season will go, or how long it will last, but it will come.
Sometimes the bulb doesn't bloom for one year,
but instead puts down its roots, feeds off the soil and earth and waits
until the right moment to appear.
The summer is here.
The flower has burst forth and stands enjoying the sun being appreciated by all.
It's beautiful, but once again none of us know apart from the bulb
what's in the soil, what's under the ground.
This bulb found a way through to get to the surface and
there it will stay until once again it's time to go to earth,
take time out and rest ready for the next spring.
We need to look after each other, look beyond the flower.
Appreciate each other for who we are, as we all have a story to tell.
Some soil is a lot deeper than others though,
And the roots grow far and wide until the time to emerge and break forth arrives.

The bulb I decided to paint is the allium it has the most amazing flower, standing tall, but reading about it, the bulb is deep in the earth.

Toxic Beauty
Lovely Laura

Dear Laura,
When you stand in front of a mirror, I know you feel the constant desire to improve yourself.

Dear Laura,
You cannot be something you're not. I know you tried hard to be what he wanted and it was always unseen or never enough.

Dear Laura,
You don't have to strive for those unrealistic standards he bullied you with. Those insecurities belong to him.

Dear Laura,
Loving yourself is giving yourself permission to like what YOU see. Forget the way he saw you with his ugly eyes.

Dear Laura,
You deserve to embrace your natural beauty and cut free from the lies you were fed.

Dear YCBD
Lovely Laura

Dear YCBD,

I just thought you should know what I'm doing. I am a woman who spends a lot of time reading, writing, teaching and healing. I am a real person, not just an object to mould.
I just thought you should know how I'm feeling. I am surviving each day, working through the pain I feel. You pushed me way too far. It's broken me apart.

I just thought you should know what I've been through since the last time I saw you. I was so hurt I moved to another city to escape the imprint of you in my mind, but you're still there. It hurts because I know you probably never cared.

I've had therapy, I'm on antidepressants, I've taken The Freedom Project, I've been in bed crying, unable to eat.

I moved to London at 28 under your false promises. I was filled with goals before I turned 30, and you turned my special time into a completely traumatic nightmare.

I just thought you should know what I wish for the future. I hope that I never meet someone as evil as you. All I want more than anything is to be okay.

I just thought you should know what I don't miss about you. I don't have to worry about you derailing my life so that your ego is boosted anymore. I don't have to be confused by your gaslighting and mood flips.

I just thought you should know what I miss a lot. I miss the woman I was before I met you. A woman who was content and safe.

I just thought you should know that you're not a man, you never were and you never will be.
It's sad that you have to lie about every facet of your existence to avoid looking like the piece of shit you truly are.

To My Younger Self
Valid Vicky

Younger self, be true, be strong,
And if you spot red flags,
Then girl, be gone.

Thank You For The Ride
Anon

Dear A,

I Just thought you should know what I'm doing now.
I am a mountain who spends a lot of time loving myself.
I'm high now, but not on your drugs.

I just thought you should know how I'm feeling.
I am bonded with self-love and commitment
Which takes me through this life's series of challenges.

I just thought you should know what I've been through;
Since the last time I saw you, I grew and grew.
But don't think that I don't need your prayers anymore.

That time I drove to London to confront you
Was especially important to me.
With that pain I sank lower than low;

114

I had to touch bedrock in order to look upwards again.

I just thought you should know what I wish for the future.
I hope that you know you won't see me at rock bottom again.
If you want to converse,
I will be up here skimming the clouds.

I just thought you should know what I don't miss about you.
I'm glad I don't have to worry about your burning fire anymore,
Which looked like a soft and calm sunset that I just had to touch.

I just thought you should know what I miss a lot.
I miss how we used to share every detail of our day.
You let me be your diary and showed me your weaknesses and secrets.
You accepted me for who I am and never asked me to change.

I just thought you should know that my mind doesn't stop.
I have to pay huge sums to calm it,
That's the price I pay for getting involved with you.
Luckily, the pockets I cultivated are deep.

Thank you for the ride.

From Me

Letter To Myself
Anon

Dear Me, when you stand in front of a mirror, what do you see that deserves such pressure? What did your body ever do to you?

Dear Me, you cannot be seriously treating this body as an enemy? It's carried you through 37 tough years and that's just presently.

Dear Me, you don't know what you have 'til it's gone, just like Joni Mitchell said, so embrace what you have till the day you're dead.

Dear Me, loving yourself is non-negotiable, you have one body and no chance to live.

Dear Me, you deserve what you have coming to you and that's all the great things that you alone can create.

Letter To Future Me
Anon

I am 47 years old, I'm the mother of a 17-year-old son who lights my life like no other.
We are connected like flowing water, taken by the wind, the riverbed and undercurrent of life.
I'm strong, I've stayed me, me is wonderful, and me is here.
My quest took me to some dark places but I never wavered.
I am a woman, you won't catch me giving up.
Broken and torn I may be, but I heal, I persist and I let the wind take me forward.
Let that storm take you where you need to go.
Ride that wave baby, the seas won't stop so learn to swim!
Look at you now and all you've achieved, you're right where you knew you'd be.

It Can Only Have Been a Miracle
Victorious Victoria

It can only have been a miracle,
Jacky and Donna coming into my life,
Into my heart,
With their mountain of Dear Friend letters.
The miracle,
The magic of the letters
From friends I didn't know I had.
Messages of love and courage,
For me,
For me!

Letters from women offering me friendship,
Acceptance,
Patience,
And courage.

The miracle of courage.
Donna says,
"You have the eye of the Tiger!".
Their love and patience is a miracle,
And makes miracles happen.

'Dear Friend Letters', To Warrior Women, From Warrior Women

Dear Wise Warrior Woman,

Looking back to week one,
Alone, confused, anxious;
Here but not, if you know what I mean.
My body,
My mind not quite sure
How I arrived here in this space.
Worried that I've taken up someone else's place,
Someone might need it more than me.
There was no violence you see,
So do I deserve to be here,
Amongst others so much in need?

As the weeks went on,
The tactics discussed each session
Shocked my system.
Like every single thing said,
Discussed,
Written,
Was naming my lived experience.

Coercive Control they called it,
So I did deserve to be there after all.
That space in that warm room,
With a sisterhood surrounding me
Like a big hug that said so lovingly,
"You will find hope."

The courage that brought you here
In week one will grow,
And before you know it

You will be celebrating completion!
Empowered,
Free,
And ready for the next stage
Of my journey with WE:ARE.
Now signed up to my next stage,
A brand new page
In my book of self-love.

Dear Wise Warrior Woman,

You entered the room,
Scared, tired, and emotional,
But you knew this was the beginning
Of your journey towards freedom.

The tears came,
And still do;
But you are no longer ashamed,
For this is your healing
And your journey towards Freedom.

There is hope,
There is kindness,
There is support,
And you are part of a sisterhood.
This is your journey towards freedom.
You are everything.
We are everything.

Dear Wise Warrior Woman,

I hope that these words find you safe and well.
I want to remind you to give yourself time
And be patient with yourself on this newfound journey.
May God bless you with endless courage to take
The first step to empowering yourself for a better future.

Welcome to the loving arms of sisterhood.

WE:ARE

We will hold you close to our hearts,
And help you on your journey to peace and freedom.
We will celebrate your small wins
And cheer you on whilst you make huge strides
In regaining your confidence and hope for a better future.

WE:ARE all so proud of you!
Keep going,
You can do this.

With much love always,
Your freedom fighting fellow Warrior Woman.

Dear Wise Warrior Woman,

When I came here I struggled to cope,
Now I sit back,
I have so much hope.
This man would never pay his maintenance,
But trust me, hold on,
You will learn patience.
He thinks he's the man of your kingdom
But you WILL get your freedom.

As you watch him gather his luggage,
You will slowly gain your courage.
As he makes all his judgement,
Let it be,
Let it go,
And learn your empowerment.

You will start to feel good;
YOU will gain your sisterhood.
As you stop the debate, you can celebrate.
As I grow and LOOK above,
I find myself and self-love.
DON'T dwell on the past,
Look forward to your future.
WE ARE all together.

Dear Wise Warrior Woman!

Thank you to me for having the courage
To come along to the freedom programme.
I have given myself hope again for a bright future.
I have made some amazing friends
With the sisterhood of freedom,
And learnt to love me again.
Me and my children are now free
To celebrate the rest of our lives.
I will always remember WE:ARE,
WE ARE AMAZING!

Dear Wise Warrior Woman,

You lived through the worst of it and survived.
You are here now,
Strengthened by your past,
And hopeful that you are going to leap forward
With renewed confidence in yourself,
And a promise to make you happy.

You are going to go easy on yourself.
Become your own best friend
Knowing that even if you get it wrong,
Your heart is in the right place,
And you don't mean harm.

You will become comfortable in your own skin,
Not seeking approval from anyone,
But knowing that it is enough
If you know in your heart that you've done your best,
Not intending wrong,
Or hurting anyone;
And have found peace in your heart.
Have hope, Wise Warrior Woman.

Dear Wise Warrior Woman,

Coming here today just shows you have been in a situation,
And now you want to be free.
Free of pain,
Free of negative thoughts,
Free of the past.

You attending the Freedom Programme
Is helping yourself to heal,
To grow and to learn,
And most of all to have peace.

Remember "Small steps, deep breaths."
WE:ARE here for you,
Your sisterhood.
In different ages,
Different colours,
Different sizes,
Empowering you with hope,
Courage and love.

Dear Wise Warrior Woman,

Hope is the thing that will bring you your freedom.
The revelation is the realisation that you don't need them.

It is ok if you don't understand
Why you had to suffer at that man's hand.
Having the courage to say ENOUGH and make that stand,
And no longer listen to his commands,
You're now a step closer to the future you'll love.
Soaring away like a free white dove

Dear Wise Warrior Woman,

WE:ARE hope,
WE:ARE freedom,
WE:ARE fighters,

WE:ARE survivors.
WE:ARE wise warrior women,
WE:ARE sisterhood,
WE:ARE the future,
WE:ARE empowered.
I am a Wise Warrior Woman.

The Freedom Programme Personas
Justice Seeking Jacky

THE BULLY tried to frighten me through banging, sulks and glares.
Wanted me to think he was angry, I was actually unaware
That these were the bully's tactics, he wasn't angry but in full control.
With freedom eyes I now realise that intimidation was his goal.
He knew exactly what he was doing, frightening me into defeat,
I'd do everything he wanted so that there wouldn't be a repeat
Of his moods, but there was, all the time.
I'd walk on eggshells, not knowing what crime
I was meant to have done, to get him so worked up
Then there came that look!
But see me now, now that I'm free,
Those dirty looks I no longer have to see.
His huff and his puffing can go to hell,
Along with his strutting, and stamping, and yells.
Goodbye to the bully, and hello to new friends,
The Freedom Programme I'd highly recommend.

THE JAILER used isolation, he said,
"You can't leave me on my own,
If you go out with your friends tonight,
You'll end up going home
With a man or two,
I know your game,
You can't help yourself,
You know you're to blame
For the fact that I have to keep track of you,
You know what you're like when you've had a few.
Your mates are all slags and you'll get a bad name,
Women who go out are whores.
You're all the bloody same.

And why does your mum always phone when I'm watching Top Gear?
Why do you whisper when your mate comes round?
Do you think that I'm stupid and can't hear....
You talking about me and making your plans
To go out and shag men when I'm not around."
With freedom eyes I now know they were tactics to keep me at home,
Away from all the friends that I had ever known,
Away from the world, isolated, alone.
Now I go out whenever I choose,
So fuck you Mr. Jailer, I win and you lose!

THE HEADWORKER used emotional abuse,
very subtlety at first so that I would excuse
His words, his actions, his behaviours, his demeanour.
Was it me? Was it him? I was none the wiser.
It doesn't hit you for a while, what they're doing to your mind,
Their aim is confusion, and it's hard to rewind
And think where it started.
The put downs and name-calling,
The making us feel worthless, useless, ugly and appalling.
It may have started with jokes, "Ha ha, where's your sense of fun?"
I laughed along at first, 'til it became humiliation.
With freedom eyes I saw that this was all planned
To break me down bit by bit, without even raising his hand.
He can't be arrested, be imprisoned, be fined,
For abusing me through controlling my mind.
With Freedom eyes, and freedom friends,
I know I'm not mad, and from now I'll defend
My right to be free, and the right to be treated with dignity.

THE BAD FATHER puts us down in front of our children.
He calls us names and makes us cry,
And thinks this doesn't hurt them.
He uses the children to make us stay with him,
Says they'll miss him if we leave, and perhaps they will.
He tells us that it's shameful to be a single mum,
And that we'd never cope on our own when he's gone.
So he uses the children to make us stay put,
Through guilt, shame, and fear, we get stuck in a rut.
Our children lose out on the innocence of childhood,
They know exactly what's happening,

No matter how hard we try to hide it.
They suffer the same isolation,
No family or friends come to stay
For visits or sleepovers, his moods drive them all away.
With no one else allowed in it gives him free reign
To carry out his abuse again and again.
No one will know what our children are going through,
We're too scared to speak out, and they won't tell you.
So we all suffer in silence until we get help to get him out,
Then through freedom eyes we realise what he's all about.
When we leave, we can finally get help for our children,
And finally tell agencies the truth and the reason
For our children's behaviour, yes no wonder they were depressed,
But they don't need a psychologist to be assessed.
They need understanding, nurturing, support and love.
They need to be listened to, believed, and have support for me, their mum.
With freedom eyes we realise what a good dad is and how he behaves,
Not an abuser, a bully, an accuser who treats us as his slaves.
Looking back now I can see his tactics,
I remember when we first met,
he told me that his one regret
Was meeting His ex, she was a bitch apparently.
Stopped him seeing his kids, and naturally
I believed him, who wouldn't, he was so convincing.
I even helped him get a solicitor so he could send her a summons
To grant him residence of his kids, she'll get her comeuppance.
In court she looked downtrodden and claimed he'd been abusive,
Pretty soon I got the same treatment,
I started to believe her, also feeling defeated.
If there's one thing to learn to spot an abuser,
He doesn't see his own kids, and his ex, he will blame her.
So run for the hills and never look back,
Cos he'll blame you next, so give him the sack.

THE KING OF THE CASTLE sits on his throne
And calls on his servants to clean up his home.
I say 'his home' with some apprehension,
Cos the words, rent, shopping and bills, are not in his comprehension,
Yet he rules his roost with an iron fist,
As he checks we've done everything on his well-prepared lists.
He makes the major decisions and we all have to agree,

No negotiation or compromise, it's all 'me me me.'
I still can't quite remember how it actually came to be,
That very quickly I had turned into a housewife from the 1950s.
That old housewives guide that we used to poke fun at
Was a reality in my house,
I'd turned into Bloody Mary Poppins.
I'd see to the kids, shop, dust, clean and cook;
But it was never enough.
He'd still moan, and shout, and complain I'd done it wrong,
Maybe he was right, maybe I was a crap mum.
That's what they want us to believe, and they tell the agencies too,
That we're unreliable, lazy, unable to see anything through.
That we can't cope on our own, that we need them there,
That we drink all day long when they're not there.
With freedom eyes we see them for what they really are.
A tyrant, a ruler, he truly thinks he's the king of the house, how bizarre.
They want praise for putting out the bins,
They think they deserve a medal for cooking a tin of beans,
They 'help us' with the housework,
They ' babysit' our kids,
Where would we be without them...heaven forbid.
It's actually a lot easier without a man like that,
These days I prefer my evenings cuddled up to my cat.

THE LIAR denies he's abusive, or says it was only a slap,
Tells us we deserved it for answering back.
He's got lots of excuses for what he does,
It's the drink, his depression, or maybe his drugs.
It's the fault of our mum, or our sister, or friend.
It's because of the work meeting we had to attend.
It's because we didn't cook his favourite dinner,
It's because his bookie didn't produce a winner.
It's because of his childhood, can't we give him a break?
It's because we don't understand him, it's because we're late.
It's everything under the sun, but he's never to blame,
No genuine remorse, no genuine "I'm sorry," not one ounce of shame.
As long as he's got a reason, he's justified it to himself,
That's why he can happily sleep at night,
Cos it's the fault of someone, or something else.
He'll justify it to anyone who'll listen,
And he'll give you all the same excuse.

Police, social workers, family, and psychiatrists,
He's out to confuse you all about his abuse.
Don't try to work them out, they do it because they can,
It's who they are, and without consequences they'll do it again and again.
Leaving them is the only way out.
Either that or a coffin,
And I'm not joking.
Two women are murdered every week,
But it's not newsworthy on Fleet Street.
Page three got more coverage than our slaughtered sisters,
No wonder we're seen as objects in a world that doesn't listen.
The rules of the game are his beliefs,
She should, she must, she can't.
And violence comes when she breaks his rules
Even though she's done nothing wrong.
How dare she, she knows that pushes my buttons,
"She drove me to it," he shouts.
All excuses, the bullshit that comes out of his mouth.
The Freedom Programme helps us see him for what he is,
A liar, an abuser, a miserable old git!

THE PERSUADER is the Oscar winning performer,
An actor worthy of the highest order.
He'll make you believe that he's as sorry as hell,
He'll cry you a river in fact he could sell
Sand in a desert, a polar bear ice.
He's a con man, a liar, and he's not at all nice.
He'll bring flowers, chocolates, and wine.
Maybe write you a poem, but not as good as mine!
You'll believe him at first, and he knows that you will,
Don't blame yourself, remember he's fine-tuned his acting skills,
He'll have done it before with his ex and he'll do it with his next.
If that doesn't work, he'll persuade us with threats,
He'll threaten to kill us, our family and our pets.
Why would we doubt him when we see on the news,
Two women a week are murdered so either way we lose.
Have him back or be killed, be silent or be silenced,
What a choice to have? And now I've got social services on my back.
He knew he was meant to stay away,
Now he's got me in trouble, and my kids will be taken away.
He doesn't even care, to him they're better out of the way.

With freedom eyes I see the persuader for what he is.
It's all about him, of course he wants to come back,
Free rent, free food, and sex on demand.
Of course he's sad, cos he's lost all control,
Making us feel guilty and feel sorry for him was his goal.
As he may get locked up for an extensive time,
He persuades us for his own needs, not mine.
With freedom eyes I see all this for the very first time.

A Survivor's Journey
Justice Seeking Jacky

Meet my new boyfriend, he's really kind,
He takes me everywhere, never leaves me behind.
He's always with me wherever I am,
He loves me, you see, my new man.
Cosy nights in just me and him,
He says we don't need no-one else to come within.
Before I knew it we were living together,
He told me I was his, forever and ever.
The signs were there early but I didn't know,
That abusive behaviour was already starting to show.
"Why do your friends visit and spoil our fun?
Why are you spending OUR money on YOUR son?
Who's that you're talking to on the phone?
What do you do all day, when I'm not at home?
Why were you at the shops for an hour?"
He was already showing his total power.

Then one night when out, I was my normal self,
Chatting and dancing, enjoying myself.
I hadn't seen my friends in oh so long,
So I tried to catch up with everyone.
Then we said our goodbyes and left for the car,
Suddenly he swung me around and threw me to the floor.
For the first time ever I was hit by a man,
Not once, or twice, but again and again.
"You slag, you tart, behave when you're out.
Get into that car!", I heard him shout.
Shock, disbelief, I didn't know what to do,

It's hard to take in when it first happens to you.
At home he cried and sobbed, and told me his tale,
Of a dreadful childhood, oh how he did wail.
Battered and abused, this poor man of mine,
So I gave him a chance, well, just this one time!

Next thing I was pregnant, he said we'd start anew,
This child would never suffer the abuse he went through;
But how they forget the promises they make,
Having him back was a big mistake.
"You'll never leave and take my son,
I'll tell Social Services you're an unfit mum.
I'll say you're a prostitute on drugs and booze"
Maybe they'll believe him and my sons I would lose.
Nothing could please him, I could do no right,
I'd leave but go back after a few nights.
What other choice did I have?
Apart from being offered a hostel, or a hard-to-let flat.
Then there were solicitors, courts, police and housing,
Too many appointments, I felt like I was drowning.
I needed someone to help me, I couldn't do it on my own,
I didn't just want to talk to a helpline on the phone.
Change your locks the housing say,
Easier said than done but how do I pay?
Months waiting for courts to set a date,
Often by then it's just too late.
See they've got to us by then, either threatening or begging,
So we retract our statements, and again forgive them.
If you read the data then you will see,
That a woman's more likely to be killed after she flees,
With this in mind and the fear set in stone
We give up, give in and go back home.

So another son later and things still looked bleak,
Apart from the days I got the odd treat,
These days would bring hope he'd shower me with gifts,
But the hope would be broken by more raging fists.
When police knocked on my door, I'd want them to stay,
But I'd pretend nothing was wrong and send them away.
It's the fear of the comebacks I'll get when they've gone,
You see he threatens to kill me if I tell anyone.

'Watch your back, I'll hunt you down,
I'll kill you one day when there's no-one around
I'll be watching you night and day
Get rid of me, No Way."

No-one saw the bruises, they were hidden away,
If I told the world I'd have hell to pay.
I felt such a fool, embarrassed, ashamed,
I thought I allowed it to happen, so I accepted the blame.
I'll leave next time he goes off his head,
If I don't do something, I'll end up dead.
Next time comes again and again, for 13 years I stood this pain
Too scared to leave, too scared to stay,
How am I going to get away?
Then the violence slowed down, no need to do it so much,
Emotional abuse had taken over his punch.
"You're stupid, ugly, cheap and scum
When I come in the door I expect my dinner to be done.
When I say jump, you'll ask "How high?"
And woe betide if I see you cry!
Don't you know how lucky you are to have me?
You'll do no better just you see.
You're late from the shops, you're lazy and fat,
Who else would look at you dressed like that?"

My spirit he tried so hard to break,
It was all I had left and it wasn't his to take.
When he started on his son with eyes full of rage,
I knew I was ready for the flight stage.
You see my eldest son died the year before
From substance abuse, he couldn't take anymore
Of his mental abuse, put downs and threats;
Now my other two children I had to protect.
When he went out, with one bag, we all fled
Walking the backstreets, if he caught me, I'd be dead.
Late that night I knocked on a friend's door,
I broke down and cried and said "No More."

Many years have now passed, it feels great to be free,
Now I help other people on their journey to recovery.
I've never looked back, our house is happy once more,

He knows I mean business, he won't come near my door.
The problem is his, I've heard he's in therapy,
At last he realises it was him that was crazy, not me.
An abusive man will never change,
So get out, get help, it's never too late.
with the right support you'll get help all the way,
and you can look forward to a bright brand-new day.
To the services out there I say cut some slack,
I know it's frustrating when you see us go back.
Put more funding in place, there's not enough here,
We need support in each area, the need is there.
Train the women who have been through the system,
They can reach those victims when services have missed them.
The University of Life is where we got our degree,
We've got more than enough for a PhD!

Dear All
Lovely Lucy

Dear all who say "Just get over it."
Or the ones who utter "Stop thinking about it."
Do you think I just sit here and have a choice in this matter?
This heart was once whole,
But each day he picked at it like he was digging dirt,
Trash.
All I ever was to him,
A body to use whenever he took time out
From his own self-indulgence to give himself all the pleasure.

Do you think I enjoy this hurt?
A deep pain,
Right inside my heart chamber,
Right next to the heart chakra,
A pain that travels right up to my throat.
Words can not access my tongue most days,
As there are no words to describe this torture.

Do you think I want to be reminded of all the names he called me?
He rewired my brain,
He gave me chills up my spine,

Each time he opened his mouth,
A mouth full of venom and lies;
But his lies were so clever that he stole my self-esteem,
Self-confidence and self-belief,
He made me believe I was living in his prison.

Dear All who say, "Let it go."
Oh I wish it were that easy,
Each day's a struggle not knowing what emotion you're up against.
Am I going to be a whirlwind tornado of sadness,
mixed into laughter?
Or maybe a bout of crying,
Tears that manifest from adrenaline,
stored in that cell of memories of name-calling.
He use to call me a snake,
He stressed me out that much that my body started to reject him,
I was covered in shedding skin, he called it;
'Cause I was that bitch who loved him.

Abuse is real,
Toxic to its very core,
People ask me, "Why didn't you leave?"
Then I say,
"Well you're still a part of this government coercion control,
It's so easy to be manipulated,
When they first feed you a cocktail of well-timed love hormones.
Evaluating you to design that trauma bond,
Get you hooked,
Using that same part of your brain,
That a drug addict feeds off.
So each time they ignore you,
Or abuse you,
You will be submissive just to get that fix,
Of how it used to be...
Them sweet names, or that loving touch.
That is long gone now.
I divorced your ass.
I stood my ground.
I am no longer an addict,
So you can take your fake ass
Off back to your crack addict,

135

You are no longer welcome here.

Dear All who have gone through this,
We are the warriors,
We don't walk around hurting others,
We do the work to heal our bleeding hearts.
One day,
Just one day,
That right love will come,
And all this ever was,
Was just a lesson to be strong and wise,
We will never be forgotten.

Safe Haven
Anon

Breathe truth, breathe lies, it's amazing how we can live a life based on falsehoods, only minimal truth is needed. I don't even need to know my name or what I'm good for. Someone will decide that for me.

The reflection I get from solitude allows the truth in. In it comes and I breathe easier, I sleep easier, my mind is my own and I live easier.

My quiet relief as I sit here takes hold of my body gradually, step-by-step I'm working on recharging. Sometimes the wire doesn't connect, doesn't reach and I run around on 10 percent But still here is my home, my safe haven, I love myself here.

Memories
Kind Kee

So my nan has been up in heaven for longer than she was in my life,
Still I hold fond memories of the perfect sister, mother, grandmother and wife.

Memories of warm milk and hot water bottles in bed,
Memories of cooking pancakes with my cousin Mark held forever in my head.

Running wild in her garden and her sliding patio doors,
She'd say "Keep ur fingers off the glass, and try not to slip on the floor!"

So we'd steam the glass with our breath and draw silly faces,
Then run down the garden again at our own pace.

Dinner time she'd shout "Come inside and sit down",
Roast dinner again with cauliflower, so I'd frown.

"Make sure you eat it all, there's children out there hungry.",
I'd mutter "Well if I don't eat it all they can have it, surely!"

Creme caramel for pudding was always on the agenda,
Never really liked it but was too scared to offend her!

Staying up late and me and Soph sharing a single bed,
"Go and have a wee," she'd say while tucking me in and kissing my head.

Morning brings cornflakes with red milk, and sugar to make it sweet.
Just push it round the bowl whilst grandad's devouring his shredded wheat.

Nan's now watching Ainsley Harriott 'Can't Cook, Won't Cook' with Sophie
on the sofa,
I'm wasting all the square note paper by the house phone trying to make
a poster.

Afternoon arrives and it's time to walk the shops,
Mooching in the charity shop and buying back her own tops!

Last minute stop at 'Absolutely Ace'
Always treated there, my new favourite place!

Nan's trolley's full so down the ramp and through the underpass,
Only reason being the shops were closing now at last!

I'm wondering now whether my nan can take the pain for much longer,
How selfish of me not to understand why she isn't stronger.

She's gone now she's left me, and escaped from the pain.
How selfish am I, 'cos I'm angry I can't see her again.

I'm hearing "Sorry for your loss," and that time's a great healer,
But time won't bring her back, let me kiss her and feel her.

Looking back now as a mother and a lady,
I am blessed to have had her hold me as a baby.

I owe you my dear nanny P for all that you gave me,
You gave me the strength, courage and determination to conquer life so bravely.

You have been up in heaven longer than you were by my side,
Take my word nanny P, in my mind, you never died.

It's A Matter Of...
Kind Kee

It's a matter of nurturing the 14-year-old me and choosing how I wish to respond...
As an adult with choices, I can give that girl her dreams and far beyond.

It's a matter of reframing healthy and unhealthy to helpful and less helpful...
It demonstrates I have always tried and makes me feel less doubtful.

It's a matter of vulnerability and not being too scared to cry...
Each teardrop is trauma leaving my body allowing the 14-year-old me to fly.

It's a matter of saying no and putting my newfound boundaries in place...
I'm not selfish, saying no is empowering and I'm protecting my space.

It's a matter of being brave enough to cross the line in my make-believe box...
Surrendered to the false security it offered, my future's now unlocked.

It's a matter of tossing away the flipping coins and now the penny's dropped...
No longer deciding heads or tails and the inner conflict's stopped.

It's a matter of reminding myself that shame is external and no possession of mine...

It has no belonging, pass it back, this reversal game takes time.

It's a matter of not absorbing what doesn't belong to me...
And leaving it right there held with whoever else it should be.

It's a matter of accepting a compliment from others and from myself...
Gaining gratitude daily and positive affirmations have excelled.

It's a matter of connection and bringing my mind and body together...
Giving myself time to unwind when I'm feeling the pressure.
It's a matter of not succumbing to others' emotional projection.
I trust in myself entirely to provide my own safety and protection.

It's a matter of being at peace with the fact that I ain't perfect...
I deserve the world and more and God knows that I am worthy.

It's a matter of realising my experiences make me unique...
They are not a reason to become my own personal critique.

It's a matter of recognising the world is mine and the sky's the limit...
There's plenty of room for personal growth and the negativity, well I can bin it.

It's a matter of thriving and dancing to the beat of my own drum...
I believe my energy has got me through and there are better things to come.

It's a matter of filling my life with self love and self compassion...
Wearing my self-worth loud and proud like it will never go out of fashion.

It's a matter of travelling through life on this journey I have just begun...
I know there will be no end but my god I believe I've already won.

It's a matter of appreciation for counsellor Annette at RSVP...
Who holds a special place in my heart and has become a part of me.

What it's really a matter of, is me...

It's a matter of me...

And don't I matter!

Thoughts
Lovely Lucy

Sometimes you have to travel alone,
To discover the pearls of wisdom and beauty,
Lying deep within the dark ocean,
Ocean of strength and no constriction.

I fly blind,
Blind to the eye,
That naked eye,
My third eye,
That eye is shy.

My thoughts are a jumble,
They like to take me to a jungle,
They swing side to side,
Pouring down streams of tears,
Guides and wisdom.

Sometimes I get lost,
Stuck,
My words can't sentence themselves,
To construct a simple sound.
My brain fog overshadows my mind,
The mind which is full of intellect,
But not accessible to comprehend
This diamond.

I tried to survive many times,
From all the lies,
Lies that made my mind,
Crazy and paranoid.

Pain held a mirror to my heart,
That piece of flesh
Kept on pumping while it was breaking.
Pain became my friend,
I embraced it,
Why not?
After all,

It saved me to move forward in my journey.
This was a new kind of crazy,
My mind was racing,
Wondering, "Where is my next dopamine hit?"
Like a drug addict,
Once I was free, but still felt caged like being in a prison,
These chains were still on me.

I discovered me,
All of me,
My soul,
My flesh,
And the skin that covers me,
My intuition runs through me,
There is no stopping me.

I am a fire,
That burning sensation of discovery.
I thought that I was going to die many times,
But now I have just had my only rebirth, that me,
Come watch me,
Stalk me,
But I will tell you one thing you will never have me,
I am reborn.

This is a self-developed me,
I love me.
I am that bird
Who can fly free whenever she chooses,
That cage has no bars or a lock,
I can perch myself,
Just watch,
Life is a blessing full of love and positivity.

Acceptance
Dani

Accept the way you look.
Accept the way you feel.
Times can be hard,

When you are mentally ill.

Pick yourself up
And brush it off,
You can't live your life
Living under a rock.

Accept you have problems,
Reach out for a helping hand.
It can be scary,
Accept as much help as you can.

Life can be a struggle,
But it's not as bad as it seems,
It's all about filling your life
With hopes and dreams.

A Tale Of The Restorative Power Of Chocolate And My Mum
Empowered Emma

Through the window
In the door,
I saw
The shiny purple box.
"I've brought you some more
CHOCOLATE!" Mum said and smiled.

"More?"
He said, "She don't need no more!
Watching her weight, ain't you, babe?
I told her she don't need to, I adore
her the way she is. But, you know what she's like!"

"It's only CHOCOLATE!" Mum said.
"Don't be a bore!"
"What am I like?" I wondered.
"Does he adore
Me?"

And I thought back to last night.

I'd lain on the floor.
Half slain, I'd wept and wailed,
Listlessly trying to claw
Some dignity back
And stop myself begging
Anymore.

His eyes of disgust
Bore
Through my skin and through
My skull, and through my brain.
My eyes were sore.
My jaw
Clenched, resistant.
He rambled on,
Through chemical breath
At four
In the morning.
Me, prey
To his carnivore.

On and on,
And on and on.
"How much of this can I endure?",
I wondered.
"Look at you! You're ugly and fat.
Everyone hates you, you know that,
right?"

"I know.",
I agreed.
It was the only way,
His paws now upon me,
Poking my face.

Then, it stopped.

I don't know when or how,
But when I was sure,
I tiptoed out of the room
And closed the door.

Fuzzy and raw,
The cortisol blinded me.

I'd crept downstairs,
and slept
On the sofa,
Cold to the core,
Unable to escape the sound
Of his snores.

And the following day, there was my Mum,
Announcing, "I've brought you some more
CHOCOLATE!".
It was like she knew.
The man she had come to abhor
Was destroying her baby's soul.
She left, frustrated,
Incapacitated,
She needed to settle the score.

A decade has past and I still hear her implore:
"Eat the CHOCOLATE!
Choose your own décor,
Get up, off the floor
Explore, be free.
You're my child, be safe, be happy.
Eat the CHOCOLATE.
Restore, restore.
Eat it galore.
Go to the seashore, get a pedicure,
The CHOCOLATE, my child,
Is a metaphor.
You. Deserve. More."

Healing
Limitless Lorraine

He had died!
My Isaac was no longer here for me to look after.
What am I going to do now?
That's all I could think about,

Shadows.

*I live in the shadows of my past.
At times breaking free when the
sun shines through.*

Every second, every minute, every hour.
What would I do to fill the void that he left?
My life was over.

I am so fucking angry!
Everyone expects me to be ok.
All I hear is "Well she still has Jordan.....she still has Renie",
Are they really that oblivious to my insufferable pain and reality?
Isaac was an individual- MY BABY!!

This 'peace and acceptance' was thrust upon me from the moment he
died,
But how could it rest easy let alone be accepted?
It's not the natural order of things to bury your child before you are gone.
To find that place of tranquillity takes years, if ever, to come.

He is now my Angel in the sky,
And I have learnt to live my life discordantly,
Much to the antipathy of others.
It's a life long journey I travel.

Shadows
Notable Naomi

I live in the shadows of my past,
at times breaking free when the sun shines through.
Like the marshmallow clouds on a bright sunny day,
suddenly blocking the sun's path.

I had a revelation today.
I had written a sentence about shadows
that I wanted to put into a picture,
but needed to check the spelling.

I quite often have thought of my life being in the shadows,
but never until today put two and two together.

Where does the light come from when shadows
have been cast over a life for so long?

So in my aim to figure out if I had the spelling under my belt...
which I hasten to add I didn't,
I stumbled upon an explanation of a shadow
which just clicked everything into place,
so I will now think of a shadow in a different light.

The light was there in the first place!

On a sunny day, you can often find a shadow.

The shadow being cast by an object in the sun's path.

In life, the shadow, quite often an object in your path
stood over your light until like a candle was snuffed out.
Enveloped in dark as in the night.

Once that object is moved
the sun can creep back into view.

The sun will always be there as will the light,
we just have to find it.

And So She Flies
Sensational Scarlett

Feathers a bloom, spectrum of colour, eye to the sky.
Honeysuckle wings they took flight, rising to the most ultimate high.

The curtains drawn, the unwritten rules, no light in the cage.
Fury, white clouds, scales, rage and fear... can anyone see, can anyone hear?

Splitting the wings inside out, redefining the feather formation.
Fragmenting into the cage, the shame, the rules etched into her for an age.

Blurred eyes, confusion, panic.
Knelt to knee asking to see, just asking please to be.

The uniforms, the bars, the children, the cage.
Lying here enraptured in pain, broken, mending. Am I, am I to blame?

Honeysuckle wings take flight to the sky, open and mending with a sigh.
A breath too quick, her chest speared with angst, she flies up high.

Honeysuckle wings of you again, they soar, they rise, they reign.

This poem is my journey, this is my truth.

I can whole-heartedly say that WE:ARE changed my whole life and that of
my daughters.

Counting Blessings
Fabulously Fearless

When counting my blessings;
I start small:
My favourite tea bags and hot water for my favourite drink.
I am grateful for my shower gel, that I get to choose;
My clean clothes and underwear that are mine alone.
I am grateful for my HRT that is getting me through this period of my life,
Even if this period will now be the only one I have.
I am grateful for a job that works around my childcare.
I am grateful for the arms of my babies that squeeze me tight
And tell me how much they love this mama I am to them.
I love that school is within walking distance and despite my aches and
pains,
I can walk to the shops and buy whatever we need.
I am grateful for this voice that seeks help; it comforts and it guides.
I am grateful for food that I can buy and don't have to grow in order to
survive.
I am grateful I learned to drive and for the freedom being able to drive
gives me.
I am grateful I learned about money from a young age;
Book wisdom, and life lessons that enable me to pay and keep our home.

I am grateful for every sunrise and sunset because no matter what happens;
These two things are a constant in my life.
Each new morning I get to try again;
At the end of each day I can lay down to rest,
Count each blessing knowing I've done my best.

Manifesting Me
Lovely Laura

When I look at my reflection I feel proud of how I got through.
I understand my worth,
The fog of abuse has dissipated,
I'm comfortable in my body.

My intuition is no longer distorted,
I'm in contact with my thoughts and feelings.
Torn between abundant paths
Of happiness to choose from.
I finally found the rock inside myself
And people I can trust to call my tribe.

Dancing like I never have before.
My crimson heels set the scene wherever I go.
Walking like the warrior woman I am and always have been.
Connected to my authentic self and at peace.
My quest to understand what he did and why,
Is something that no longer plagues my mind.

Time Is A Gift
Victorious Victoria

Time is a gift for me and my daughter.
I have drunk the clear, icy water and have woken up.
It's been hard to loosen my grip, to exhale,
To let her go, as far as the end of my arms,
To see her.
I'd been hoping for survival,
Cowering, holding her tight,
Holding my breath.

Yesterday I saw her,
Beautiful, calm, happy, alive –
Her own self.
Taller than ever and smiling at me, eye to eye.
Tomorrow is completely new.
Today, I can go to bed and sleep,

I am safe and free.
She is safe and free.

On Gratitude
Anon

When counting my blessings I start small,
I never take a good night's sleep for granted.
My warm bed gives me a loving hug each night
And is the rock of peacefulness to which I cling.

Holding my baby,
Who shows me love in everything he does.
I'm grateful he is secure enough
To show me anger and give me harsh words;
I cherish that rawness as much as the love.
Women who show me the truth about life and love;
I hold them up for clearing the path,
Lighting the dark corners and pushing me
To have the courage to say no (and for putting the kettle on).
My secret love affair with chocolate deserves a mention:
It will never talk shit about me,
The way I talk,
Or tell me to smile.

Counting Blessings
Real Rachel

When I count my blessings I start small,
From that pregnancy test you grew and grew inside of me,
Listening to my heartbeat from the inside, wriggling while I sleep.
Then you came, my miracle.
You were born with 10 tiny toes, 10 little fingers,
And one beautiful cute nose.
A day old, a week, a month, a year.
You grow and so does my blessing.
He may have helped create you,
He may claim some sort of ownership,
Oh yes that play Dad, who picks and chooses,

But ultimately blessing, you are mine.
We grew stronger together,
And yes, blessing,
Yes, you are mine!

A Peaceful Place
Justice Seeking Jacky

A peaceful place, A smiling face, A warm embrace
Peace sounds like the waves on the sea, calm after the storm, relaxing music, the birds in the trees, a summer's breeze
Peace Feels like a soft pillow, new sheets, a cosy duvet, welcoming you into a restful sleep,
Peace tastes like sweet nothings, cream in coffee, ice cream sundaes, a box of chocs and scotch on the rocks
Peace takes time and patience, don't rush, don't judge your journey by someone else's, piece-by-piece you will get there
Peace leaves a warm taste in my mouth, a calming feeling in my body, positive thoughts in my head, my body and brain working in harmony
Peace is mine to behold
So do not disturb
It has taken a long time to get here and it's not going anywhere
I'm maintaining my peace
My trauma's released
My wish for you is to find your peaceful place, a smiling face and a warm embrace

Instructions For Peace
Justice Seeking Jacky

1) Play your favourite music soft or loud, dance like you're proud of your body, your moves, strut your stuff till you feel the power of rhythm running through your skin
2) Stay in the bath for as long as you can manage, keep running the hot water to your heart's content.
3) Join a book club, read a new book once a month, gain the knowledge, your brain will thank you for your newfound enlightenment
4) Caress someone everyday, someone who is worthy of your love, a

partner, a pet or even yourself. Enjoy the release of oxytocin to dilute your stress hormones

5) Watch the sunrise with someone you love, or in solitude, both are cool

6) Make soup, a big pot and freeze some so you don't have to cook for a week

7) Breathe through your stomach, relax and let it go

8) People watch, sit quietly watching the world go by and get lost in your thoughts.

9) Nap when you can, even if it's for a few minutes, the world can wait while you take some time for yourself

10) Don't stay on the phone too long if the conversation is draining your battery, your phone battery and/or your brain battery, they both need a break

11) Speak Truth to Power whenever you get the chance, your voice matters

12) Join in peaceful protests, hold your banner high, sing, chant, dance with those who have the same passion, determination and fighting spirit as you.

Instructions for Peace
Fabulously Fearless

1) Run yourself a lovely relaxing bath.

2) Put your hand on your heart and breathe.

3) Put on your favourite playlist and settle down for a good long soak.

4) Now you're relaxed, remember the power you have over how you feel.

5) Drink a tall glass of ice-cold water.

6) Refresh your mind, body and soul with soothing caresses of gentle, kind and loving words.

7) Embrace your solitude like the sun as it rises over the horizon.

8) Banish those negative thoughts running over and over in your mind.

9) Rinse and repeat as often as you can.

10) Keep this list somewhere safe, like your peace, it all comes from within.

Peace Takes Time
Courageous Carly

Peace is waking up in the morning with a happy heart
Peace sounds like laughter, happy voices and excitement
Peace feels like warmth, calmness and tranquillity
Peace tastes like satisfaction, calmness of the senses
Peace takes time, self-awareness and self-dedication
Peace leaves trauma behind, shuts the door to abuse
Peace is where I want to be and what I strive to have
Peace is freedom from the noise.

A Taste Of Peace
Super Sara

Peace is being content with who I am and what my future will be.
Peace sounds like the sound of waves and birds chirping in my ears.
Peace feels like a warm comforting hug and the feeling of being safe at home.
Peace tastes like a hot meal I have been longing for from my mother.
Peace takes who I was and shows me who I am destined to be.
Peace leaves me feeling reborn and ready for a new life of hope and happiness.
Peace is where my heart and soul feel free and finally home.

A Purse Full Of Peace
Anon

Peace is a purse full of pieces of freedom.
Peace sounds like the echo from the break in the arrow you just shot.
Peace feels like the candle being lit, with my memories of your frustration, trying to jump start the pinball wizard machine. Your coins don't fit in, and you don't know why, but I do.
Peace tastes like hot custard poured over chaos crumble. My tongue is cold now, after forced fire eating, as your main circus attraction.
Peace takes away the tears of ghosts – now smiling at the souls of the crime scene, knowing they are just passing through, and not stopping to pick up new friends.

Peace leaves.. swept up, still dancing in all their colours. Not being crunched underfoot, by the fear-sledge of rubble,
Peace is the medicine created by currency.
Bottled crystal drops, made from the icicles that melted over the safety of the fire pit ashes.

Instructions For Peace
Anon

Never. Never ever throw up your power from drinking toxic soup.
Caress the music that rises in the steam from your bath.
Don't let your solitude run cold.
Keep running the hot tap.
And afterwards stay grounded.
Soak up the goodness with big husks of bread, dipped in the sunrise of the soul soup of the choices you made.

Peace
Sensual Sarah

Peace is inevitable if you let it be
Peace is on the horizon, my horizon
Peace sounds like calm, I can breathe easy
Peace sounds like the patter of raindrops
Peace feels like I am enveloped in loving harmony
Peace tastes like ecstasy and golden honey
Peace takes away pain
Peace takes acceptance that I am worth more, I am worth PEACE
Peace leaves us full
Peace is mine

Peace
Kickass Katie

PEACE is Freedom, it's untying the straitjacket
PEACE sounds like your comfort programme on TV
The text notification on your phone, a new number, a new ringtone

PEACE feels like your new skincare products and your hair freshly cut and dyed.
PEACE tastes like your favourite spicy food that you can fully eat in peace- the whole thing all to yourself!
PEACE takes the tight chest away
PEACE leaves deep slow breaths in its place
PEACE is realising, it's over!

Peace
Anon

Peace feels like heaven , a warm glow of happiness and safety in abundance and the biggest ever embrace.
Peace tastes like cream on a fruited scone with strawberry jam and a nice cup of tea. Maybe a cucumber sandwich too!
Peace takes me to places I want to be. Peace takes all my worries and fears away. Peace takes my anxiety and gives me strength.
Peace leaves healing, strength and the ability to love myself. Peace leaves an imprint and impression of how new things should be. Peace leaves thoughts that calm and nurture recovery.
Peace is a dream, me and my family.
Peace is having a voice, having space for my thoughts, feeling happy and not feeling terrified.
Peace sounds like a sunny day in Spain, the buzzing noise you get, water gently moving on the pool, a far away road, the breeze that flickers, the leaves and the sways of the palm trees, my breath.

How Do You Know You Are On The Right Track?
Valid Vicky

It's in the way you hold yourself,
Walking taller,
Feeling more sure.

It's in the way you consider your options,
And to not being bullied any more.

It's in the way your hair stands on end
When others' words ring true.

It's in the way those warrior women
Are always there for you.

Thank you warrior women xXx

Two Jackets, A Haircut And Lunch!
Justice Seeking Jacky

This jacket is a reminder of the cruel tactics abusers use to win us back from the safety of refuge.

"Remember that jacket you always wanted, son. Meet me in town with your mum
and it's yours"
We left the refuge full of hope
My 10-year-old son happy with the promise of a new coat
Another chance maybe?
A sudden change in his personality!
We got on the bus and the two of us set off to town
He was there waiting right on time
With a smile
Happy to see us
He led us to the shops
But first, a stop off
At the barbers
Nice new haircut for my son
Two treats,
he'd won
us over
Then we chose our new jackets
Yes, me too
Aren't we lucky we thought
It's wasn't often he bought
Us anything
Then off to lunch
It's funny how you forget the bad times
The put downs, rages and the last punch
that sent us fleeing to refuge with cases packed and no going back
And there we sat eating lunch
Together

His forever
He tells us
Today the past is behind us
No more cries or lies or bad times
My son has a new haircut,
a new jacket and the promise of a good life if we return home
That night we left the refuge so that he didn't have to spend another night alone
So you see, It didn't take much to forget the last punch,
A haircut, two jackets and lunch!
A bribe, a prize, a gift,
Erased cruel words and raging fists
This jacket is a reminder of how persuasion won
And a distant memory of my much missed son

Instructions For Peace
Limitless Lorraine

You have the POWER to do this!
Your stomach can take this!
So enjoy your comforting warm bowl of soup; you deserve it!
In your SOLITUDE you will see the SUNRISE, feel free, fly high in the sky like a bird
Be CARESSED as you envelop yourself into a cold then hot running bath swamped by bubbles; your calming music playing in the background as flickering candles illuminate the room
It's YOUR TIME FOR PEACE

To 22-Year-Old Me
Empowered Emma

Hey, you. It's me.
Where's your sparkle?
Where's it gone?
I used to see it shine,
Beam from your eyes,
Radiate form your smile.

But, it's gone.

It went slowly.
A drop at a time.
Diminished.
Vanished.
Abolished.
He took it, removed it.
Slowly, deliberately, tactically.
A tiny bit at a time, so you wouldn't notice.

But I notice.
I see you.
I hear you.

Thank you. Thank you for noticing.
Thank you for seeing.
Thank you for hearing.
Thank you for validating.
Am I OK?

Not yet.

Will I be OK?

My darling, you will.
You will soar, you will rise, you will fly.

How?

A tiny bit at a time.
You'll replenish
re-establish
nourish
re-furnish
embellish
You'll accomplish.

You will grow.

He will stop me.

No, warrior, you're unstoppable.

Am I?
Yes.

Are you sure?

I know.

Do you?

You will thrive.

Can I? Will I?

You will. You are.
Your feet are firm.
Feel the rotation of the earth.
Feel the warmth of the sun.
Breathe in the air.
It's your turn.

If Escaping Was An Olympic Sport
Valid Vicky

You jumped higher than anyone thought possible,
With the weight of the world on your shoulders.
You ran faster than you have ever run before,
Whilst being dragged back by the bonds of trauma.
You lifted the little ones high for as long as you could,
To protect their innocence from the dangers all around them;
And each time you dived into the unknown,
You held your breath,
And tried not to make a splash
or the slightest ripple that he would notice.
If escaping domestic abuse was an Olympic sport,
My friends,
You would all be on track for team gold.

My Story
Empowered Emma

This is my story.
My story.
Not his.
Mine.
I'll write it. Me.
Give me that pen.
I'll take my pencil back.
That's my typewriter.
Get your hands off. It's mine.

You don't get to tell these lies.
I know that they are all desperate to listen, that they all want to hear you.
They are desperate to raise themselves by lowering me. They gather.
Baying.
They are gleeful.
They rejoice.
They gain through their sick vicariousness.
Society loves an underdog.
Except if the underdog is a woman.
Then, they want to hear his lies. Not her truth.
His lies are ugly, but her truth is uglier.
Too ugly to admit to.

Instead, they pretend.
They chide.
Join in the eye-rolling, feigned exasperation.
They want to contribute, exaggerate.
Laugh.
Scowl
Judge
Sneer.

"What is wrong with her?!" they joyfully ask one another.
It makes them feel good, confirms their twisted world view.

But this is my story. Not his, not theirs.
My story.
Not his. Mine.

Change
Notable Naomi

Thrown into a hole
Dark and deep
Damp and cold

A blanket of soil
No light
Silent

In the silence came security
Time and nourishing

Growth
Life
Joy

Bursting forth into daylight
Escape and freedom
Beauty
Sun
Wind
Rain

Life.

To Myself 10 Years On
Valid Vicky

Beautiful woman,
Cherish your lines,
They reflect how far you've come in your time.
Clever she-wolf,
Worldly and wise,
The young ones look up to you with innocent eyes.
Fun-loving female,
No more trouble or strife,
Finally there, living YOUR best life.
Independent woman,

Look how far you've come,
You're happy and healthy and THE number one.

Freedom is...
Jolly Jamie

Like walking outside, able to breathe the crisp fresh air,
all without feeling in the depth of despair.
Like happiness exploding across your body,
allowing you to see, to feel, to be calm and be present.
Like tasting the most amazing dish on the planet.
Like crystal clear air with a fresh smell,
like a bouquet of flowers, so far from hell.
Colourful and bright, filled with delight.
The feeling of freedom is simple for me,
it's to wake up in the morning and just feel free.

Peace Is
Fabulously Fearless

Peace is what I have finally found. All those years raging and arguing with brick walls; mom was right. Walk away, they don't deserve you, they never have and they never will.
Peace is what I was looking for.
Peace sounds like the running water for that well-deserved hot bath; the dawn chorus as the birds awaken to a glorious new day. Peace sounds so good on me.
Peace feels like a fleeting moment; like butterflies and dandelion seeds floating through the sky. Peace feels like the first kiss of the warm sun on your skin after the winter is finally over; it feels like the jewels of my children's embrace as they hold me close.
Peace tastes like the best cup of tea in the world, ever; like a refreshing glass of water at the breaking of the fast, quenching my thirst for life.
Peace takes a long time; so relax, take your time; don't rush. Smell the roses, feel the rain; peace will still be waiting.
Peace leaves often but she hasn't gone very far, she's right around the corner waiting patiently for me. I miss her so much, I am trying to keep her forever this time.
Peace is everything I ever needed and wanted. All these years I believed it resided outside of me but she's been here inside me all along.

Peace is beautiful and serene.
Peace is gratitude and love; all wrapped up inside of me.
I AM peace and peace IS me.

If Freedom Were...
Justice Seeking Jacky

If Freedom were a colour
It would be purple, white and green,
On sashes, flags and banners those colours could be seen.
Colours worn with pride symbolising dignity, purity, and hope,
The Suffragette movement campaigned so that women could vote.
Women died, women were imprisoned,
Women campaigned so that others would listen.
With these colours we remember
Those who showed no fear,
Those who stood their ground
For a cause held so dear.

If Freedom was a person,
She would be a woman
Holding her banner high.
Proudly,
Revolutionary,
In solidarity
With her sisters worldwide,
Demanding an end to violence against women and girls.
She would not be afraid to speak out,
To Challenge society,
To Challenge the powers that be
Who reinforce the abusers' beliefs;
The law. The media. Religion. Culture.
She would challenge those agencies
who blame the victim,
Whilst abusers get off scot-free
With no further action.
She will not be silenced
By those in power
Dressed in expensive suits,
Sitting In their ivory towers.

If Freedom were a superhero
She wouldn't be a Disney Princess,
She wouldn't need to be saved by a Prince.
She'd be every woman in our group,
Every woman who's survived abuse,
Every woman who stands up and shouts,
'Domestic abuse, stamp it out.'

If freedom were a song it would be lyrics from,
Joan Armatrading,
Tracey Chapman,
Helen Reddy,
All rolled into one.
It would be sung with a passion
From deep down inside,
Each word would give a feeling
Of hunger and pride,
We'd sing it out loud,
In our houses, on the streets;
And hope that our collective voices would reach
All of you out there so you'd all hear the message,
We are women, we are strong and don't ever forget it.

If Freedom was a last text
It would say you have the right to be happy,
You have the right to be free,
I know how you're feeling
Because that once was me.
None of this is your fault,
You are not to blame,
He was abusive before you met him,
Controlling women is his game.
Get help before he kills you,
Before he grinds you down,
Reach out and talk to someone,
When you're ready, I'll be around.

I know what Freedom looks like,
Cos freedom is me.

Shout Out Freedom
Justice Seeking Jacky

We shout out freedom from our hearts
Today's a brand new start
With voices loud and strong
Come join us in on our song

When we all sing together
No one can bring us down
Waving arms in the air
Stating we now wear the crown

WE ARE strong
We are brave
We are hopeful
We are great
We are ourselves
We are a team
We are our new-found self-esteem
We are proud
We are loud
We are knowledge abound
We are me
We are you
We are here for you too

Empowering each other
With words, rhymes and song
Educating those services who have done so many wrong
Striving each day to help them understand
The strength and courage it takes
to reach out for freedom's hand

At times, the road may seem so long
And you'll feel deflated and alone
That's when freedom friends and song
Will reawaken your creative soul
Find your freedom my friend
We are waiting here for you
sing out for every woman
To rise, reclaim, recover too

I Am Looking At You Miss Yankey
Lovely Lucy

I am looking at you,
All that sass and glare,
Yes that's right,
All in one stare,
You stand there,
Liberating,
With your words of passion,
Imposing a divine infusion,
Wanting a heart to take action,
A soul to unchain,
A rewiring to some degree,
so we won't be lost,
In that,
Far stretch disassociation,
From our own eternal dignity.

I am looking at you,
All that sweet sugar coating all over your body,
Them frosted freckles sprinkled to the right degree,
To give the sightseer a foretold note,
That you are a special delivery,
A smile that creates a happy atmosphere,
Each spirit in your company is lucky,
Lucky like a manifestation of a high level of consciousness,
To know how just to be,

I am looking at you,
Filled with all that energy,
Some days may be a struggle,
But just know each time you show up,
You touch so many lives with all your positivity.

I am looking at you,
To reach greater depths,
That honey mouth,
Words with a dash of salt,
Some need to hear the sweetest of glamour,
Mixed with a bitter taste,

WE:ARE

To know the duality,
Of hope and fear.

I am looking at you,
I speak for the eyes and ears,
Casting my vision,
The expression you imprint upon another,
Leaves an ability to unfold,
Emotions and accessibility,
Never forget your worth,
Even in that darkest hour,
You are that lamp,
In that midst,
Of humanity.

POETRY PRESCRIBED:

Since launching Poetry Prescribed in 2017, Miss Yankey has connected with thousands of people, most of whom possess little to no writing experience. Miss Yankey takes pride in supporting people to explore their own creative abilities, and in turn to express their thoughts and feelings confidently. Miss Yankey's workshops promote the therapeutic benefits of Spoken Word and creative writing and provide valuable self-management tools. She believes that equipping people with the ability to express themselves in a healthy and creative way not only boosts confidence, but can also positively affect their long term mental health and wellbeing.

Miss Yankey has a breadth of experience having worked with organisations including BBC Radio London, London's City Hall, Royal College of Psychiatrists, Birmingham University, Rethink, Youth Realities, Women and Girls Network, London Academy of Excellence, and Mind. Poetry Prescribed have facilitated workshops to children and young people in both educational and social settings, corporate organisations looking to promote creative thinking and writing for wellbeing, community mental health services (CAMHs) seeking therapeutic activity for service users, women's groups and organisations wanting to provide safe spaces for their service users to express, and many more. Miss Yankey has held over 100 workshops covering a wide variety of subject matter available including: 'An Introduction to Spoken Word,' 'Writing Slam Poetry,' 'Writing Affirmations and Setting Intentions,' 'Discussing Mental Health,' 'Culture of Violence,' 'Surviving Loss,' 'Pursuit of Happiness,' 'Sisterhood, Self-care and Creation,' plus many more.

To find out more please get in touch, or visit www.poetryprescribed.co.uk

Testimonials

"Poetry Prescribed allowed me to reflect on what I had been through, how I once felt, how I have progressed, and to focus on where I want to be. Using poetry/spoken word allows you to say how you feel frankly, without needing an explanation, without being questioned, without thinking too hard about why you got here. It allowed me to build acceptance that I am where I am at this point and draw strength from the fact that I have a shared experience with others in the group."

"Miss Yankey's workshops are a safe space to explore as little or as much as you feel comfortable to do. The option to share if you want to was much needed and those of us that did, opened the door for others to feel comfortable to do the same, or just hold space and provide comfort and reassurance that we were there, and it was safe. It also helped bring to the surface so much that has been buried or denied for a long long time. It gave a voice to our souls to speak their truth. I am forever indebted and lightened of the burdens I have carried for way too long."

"I think these workshops really support women. I don't like the way the government has made us say gender based violence. The majority are male perps and it's mainly WOMEN who get abused. I think it helps us see what happened to us doesn't mean that we will always be "victims." I hate this word also. It helps us to verbalise our traumas in a way that nobody else would understand. The workshops helped us see that it was never us or anything we ever did. I really believe this poetry course has turned me into more than a survivor. I am thriving. It's given me hope for a better future, and I now happily choose to challenge myself."

"Poetry Prescribed brought a group of women together to share their creativity and experiences in a safe and open space, and it has been an amazing thing to be a part of. The things I have learnt during these sessions have equipped me with new coping mechanisms going forward."

"A platform to be heard and release difficult emotions in a safe place. I can't think of how else I would have released what I did."

"The workshops were amazing. They were well thought through, and there was so much content, examples of poetry for inspiration in writing our own, but also an inspiration for reflection and growth."

"I think Poetry Prescribed should get funding to help as many women as possible. Domestic abuse is through the roof, and we have no safe sanctuary, but at these workshops, I felt I could express myself throughout. Thank You Miss Yankey, as you have opened a whole new page for me. I don't stop writing now."

"The course was amazeballs. Miss Yankey was outstanding. The WhatsApp group was a fantastic idea. Now we all come together and benefit each other. I think because she has been through trauma like we have, it really worked even more. If that was a social worker doing the course, nobody would have said a word."

WE:ARE - Supporting Women to Rise Reclaim Recover

WE:ARE a small survivor-led charity who have been working in the field of domestic abuse in Birmingham for 21 years. We deliver a pathway of awareness, empowerment and parenting programmes alongside a range of creative activities and volunteering opportunities.

The programmes we deliver are as follows:

10-week 'Our Healing Home' programme helps mothers safely explore the impact domestic abuse has had on themselves and their children and explores strategies for healing and repairing the relationship which has been undermined and sabotaged by the perpetrator. Weekly sessions consist of a range of group discussions, exercises and videos and further activities to do at home with their children.

11-week 'Freedom Programme' explores the abusive tactics, controlling behaviours and belief systems of the personas of the dominator and the effects on women and children's health and well-being. The end of each session studies the non-abusive counterpart looking at what a relationship built on equality and respect looks and feels like.

12-week 'Own My Life' is an innovative, creative and educational 12-week course. It supports women in regaining ownership of their lives when they have been subjected to abuse or violence by a partner. This is done through short videos, structured discussions, group and individual activities, and a comprehensive learning journal.

With more research available on the effects of living under a regime of power and control there is an increasingly growing need to put in place strategies and programmes to ensure the healing and rebuilding process is not left out when looking at preventative strategies. We recognise the long term and pervasive impact of domestic abuse and the need for a safe space to be able to process and express what has happened and to have those experiences validated. The need for longer term funding to ensure safe, consistent, nurturing relationships and environments is all the more evident so that women can heal and thrive. Successful outcomes teach us that with the right support, domestic abuse does not have to mean a life sentence for women and children and that recovery and healing is possible. *- Jacky, Donna & Kirsty*

Website: http://weareuk.org
Twitter: @dvsouthbham
Facebook: www.facebook.com/weare.dvsouthbham
Instagram: @rise.reclaim.recover
YouTube: https://www.youtube.com/channel/
UCswfnXrP_6M7PfwWxKG0flg (Dear Friend Letter Videos)

WE:ARE Art Group

All of the wonderful art published in this book was created by the WE:ARE art group, led by cover artist, Hopeful Holly.

WE:ARE art group is a sanctuary for warrior women and survivors coming together in a supportive and empowering environment to explore the healing power of art. This transformative community is designed to provide a safe space where participants can freely express their emotions, triumphs, and personal journeys through artistic endeavours.

WE:ARE art group cultivates a rich exploration of emotions, memories, and thoughts that may be difficult to articulate with words alone.

Moreover, the collective strength of this community fosters a sense of solidarity and understanding among the participants. The warrior women and survivors in this group find solace in connecting with others who have gone through similar experiences, creating an atmosphere of compassion, empathy, and shared resilience.

The regular gatherings provide a consistent platform for members to support one another through sharing personal stories, reflecting on their progress, and offering constructive feedback. These interactions often spark a sense of collective healing, encouraging each individual to embrace their personal growth and celebrate their artistic achievements.

WE:ARE art group values the therapeutic aspect of art as a means of self-discovery and healing, aiming to empower each participant on their unique journey toward personal transformation. Through artistic expression, individuals can tap into their inner strength, uncover hidden emotions, and learn to embrace their experiences with courage and resilience.

"I look forward to joining the art sessions every week. I really enjoy the art we do with our very talented teacher, Holly. More importantly it makes me feel relaxed and happier. I feel very supported by Holly and all the group participants and it's so nice to be able to help support other group members too. We are a very close group, all having suffered domestic abuse in all its forms. Not that we discuss that, nor that there's any notion that we should or need to, but the general support and knowledge we've all been or are in the same position is so amazingly helpful and valuable. There's no pressure on us whatsoever, but we all share the same love for art." - Warrior Woman

"The process of making art together is so very therapeutic and calming. Holly is the most wonderful teacher. She is so positive and helpful, as well as being a truly talented artist. She finds subjects for us every week, which she paints and prepares for us by sketching out the basic shapes and elements, or we can draw or paint what we want. She also demonstrates how to do things if we want. I would really miss our sessions." - Warrior Woman

"WE:ARE art group is more than just painting to me. It's about having someone to talk to, to interact with, to try and not be in that space of anxiety. Most weeks Holly's art group is the only time I speak to people and I find it hard to do it then. I have complex PTSD from domestic violence and I find the action of painting helps my brain calm down, my body Feel safe, and my nervous system a chance to heal. Holly (art teacher) is such an amazing and patient kind caring lady we are very blessed to have her... she gives us various levels of stuff to do depending on how poorly we are. It's such a loving and caring little art community I feel like I can just be myself. We do all kinds of art from watercolour to college to mixed media. Doing painting is the thing that I have found most healing during my healing journey. It has really helped me and I am so grateful to WE:ARE for helping me and being there for me." - Warrior Woman

HELPFUL CONTACTS

All resource links and contact information were tested and valid at time of writing. Changes may occur and links may break. Publisher apologises for any inconvenience.

BIRMINGHAM SERVICES

Birmingham and Solihull Women's Aid
- early intervention, advice and support at our drop-in centres
- emergency refuge housing
- housing support and advice
- a confidential domestic abuse helpline

Contact details
- Telephone: 0808 800 0028
- Lines open: Every day 9:15am to 5:15pm
- Website: www.bswaid.org
- Visit: Early Intervention Hub - Bank House, 36 Bristol Street, Birmingham B5 7AA
- Drop in: Monday and Tuesday 10:00am to 4:00pm, Wednesday 1:00pm to 4:00pm, Thursday and Friday 10:00am to 4:00pm

Anawim
- support with housing, mental health, finances, and access to legal aid
- counselling services
- courses
- webchat

Contact details
- Telephone: 0800 019 8818

- Website: https://anawim.co.uk/

Bharosa Domestic Abuse

- culturally appropriate and sensitive support to women aged 16+ experiencing domestic abuse from a South Asian background
- DV awareness, Safeguarding, Healthy & Unhealthy Relationships, Confidence Building, Anxiety & Stress.
- provides support in a range of different languages including Bengali, Urdu, Punjabi, Mirpuri and Gujarati

Contact details

- Telephone: 0121 303 0368
- Lines open: Monday to Thursday 9:00am to 5:00pm and Friday 9:00am to 4.00pm
- Email: bharosa@birmingham.gov.uk

Birmingham LGBT Centre

- independent domestic violence advocate service
- crisis intervention
- safety planning
- support for those experiencing or at risk of honour-based violence or forced marriage
- The Rainbow Project - eight week programme for lesbian, bisexual and trans women who are experiencing, or have experienced domestic abuse

Contact details

- Telephone: 0121 643 0821
- Lines open: Monday to Friday 9:00am to 11:00pm and Saturday 11:30am to 7:00pm
- Email: idva@blgbt.org
- Website: www.blgbt.org

Cranstoun

- help adults and young people facing difficulties with domestic abuse, alcohol, drugs, housing and criminal justice
- assessment and support for victims and children
- assessment and support for those engaged in abusive behaviour
- support for survivors

Contact details

- Telephone: 0121 633 1750
- Lines open: Monday to Friday 9:00am to 5:00pm
- Email: birminghamadmin@cranstoun.org.uk

- Website: www.cranstoun.org

Birmingham Crisis Centre
- supported safe housing
- counselling services

Contact details
- Telephone: 0121 507 0707
- Lines open: 24 hours, 7 days a week
- Website: www.birminghamcrisis.org.uk

Gilgal Birmingham
- supported safe housing
- practical and emotional support for women and children

Contact details
- Telephone: 0800 008 6622
- Email: mail@gilgalbham.org.uk
- Website: www.gilgalbham.org.uk

GreenSquareAccord
- emergency short-term housing
- floating support
- help with securing a new long-term home
- help with legal advice, as well as accompanying you to appointments and court

Contact details
- Telephone Number: 0121 358 9052
- Email: fernbrookestaff@greensquareaccord.co.uk
- Website: www.greensquareaccord.co.uk

Roshni
- specialist support to victims of forced marriage, so-called 'honour' based abuse, and female genital mutilation (FGM)

Contact details
- Telephone: 0121 643 0301 - different languages available
- Lines open: 24 hours, 7 days a week
- Website: www.roshnibirmingham.org.uk

RSVP
- emotional support and information for dealing with the effects of rape and sexual violence
- information about social groups, advocacy, and counselling

Contact details
- Telephone: 0121 643 0301
- Website: www.rsvporg.co.uk
- Email: info@rsvporg.co.uk

Sikh Women's Aid
- confidential, empathetic and non-judgmental person centred emotional support
- information to help you understand your rights and make informed decisions.
- Support to access legal support

Contact details
- Telephone: 0333 090 1220
- Email: info@sikhwomensaid.org.uk
- Website: https://www.sikhwomensaid.org.uk/

The Salvation Army
- supported safe housing
- self-help support

Contact details
- Telephone: 0121 236 6554
- Email: williambooth.birmingham@salvationarmy.org.uk
- Website: www.salvationarmy.org.uk/domestic-abuse

Horizon Sexual Assault Referral Centre
- Free, confidential healthcare and compassionate support, in Birmingham, Coventry and Wolverhampton (West Midlands) to adults (18 years and older) and young people aged 16 and 17 (if clinically appropriate) who have experienced sexual assault, including rape.

Contact details
- Telephone: 0330 223 0099
- Email: horizon.sarc@nhs.net
- Website: https://horizonsarc.org.uk/

The Waiting Room
- directory for health and wellbeing services across Birmingham and Solihull

Contact details
- Website: www.the-waitingroom.org

Trident Group
- domestic abuse helpline
- emergency refuge and long term supported housing
- help for female rough sleepers
- housing and floating support services for women and men with children

Contact details
- Telephone: 0800 111 4223
- Lines open: Monday to Friday 9:00am to 5:00pm
- Email: BhamDAreferrals@tridentreach.org.uk
- Website: www.tridentgroup.org.uk

Women Acting in Today's Society (WAITS)
- refuge and financial support
- counselling
- support for offenders

Contact details
- Telephone: 0121 440 1443, extension 103
- Email: office@waitsaction.org
- Website: www.waitsaction.org

UK SERVICES

24-hour Freephone National Domestic Violence Helpline (Refuge)
https://www.nationaldahelpline.org.uk/
As a woman fleeing domestic abuse, you may want to access specialist refuge accommodation. The Helpline can help you find a refuge vacancy for you and your children; call us for more information. We can also support you to find other specialist services in your community, which can provide support whether or not you have left your partner.
Phone: 0808 2000 247
Refuge Tech Safety: https://refugetechsafety.org/

Asian Women's Resource Centre
https://www.ashiana.org.uk/about/
Empowers Black & Minority Ethnic women, particularly South Asian, Turkish and Middle Eastern women and girls with culturally sensitive advice, support and safe housing - enabling them to make positive and appropriate choices for themselves.
Phone: 020 8539 0427
Email: info@ashiana.org.uk

BAWSO
https://bawso.org.uk/en/
Bawso provides practical and emotional prevention, protection and support services to Black Minority Ethnic (BME) and migrant victims of Domestic Abuse, Sexual Violence, Female Genital Mutilation, Forced Marriage, Honour Based Violence, Modern Slavery and Human Trafficking.
Phone: 02920 644 633
Email: info@bawso.org.uk

Childline
https://www.childline.org.uk/
Lines open: 24 hours a day, 7 days a week
If you're a child looking for confidential help
Phone: 0800 1111

Elder Abuse Hourglass
https://wearehourglass.org/
For victims of elder abuse.
Our helpline is entirely confidential and free to call from a landline or mobile, and the number will not appear on your phone bill. Our helpline and chatbot are available 24/7. All other services are open Monday to Friday, 9am to 5pm.
Phone: 0808 808 8141
Email: enquiries@wearehourglass.org
Text: 07860052906

FLOWS | Finding Legal Options for Women Survivors
https://www.flows.org.uk/
FLOWS support women to protect themselves from violence, gain court orders, access legal aid and navigate court processes.
Phone: 0203 745 7707, phone line available Monday to Friday, 9am to 5pm. Email: flows@rcjadvice.org.uk

Forced Marriage Unit
https://www.gov.uk/stop-forced-marriage
Contact the Forced Marriage Unit (FMU) if you're trying to stop a forced marriage or you need help leaving a marriage you've been forced into.
Telephone: 0207 008 0151, Monday to Friday, 9am to 5pm
Out of hours: 020 7008 1500

From overseas: +44 (0)20 7008 0151
Email: fmu@fcdo.gov.uk

FORWARD (Foundation for Women's Health Research and Development)
https://www.forwarduk.org.uk/
FORWARD is the leading African women-led organisation working to
end violence against women and girls, including access to FGM specialist
clinics.
Phone: 0208 960 4000
Email: support@forwarduk.org.uk

Galop - the LGBT+ anti-abuse charity
https://galop.org.uk/
Emotional and practical support for LGBT+ people experiencing domestic
abuse.
Monday – Thursday, 10am to 8pm
Friday, 10am to 4:00pm
Phone: 0800 999 5428
Email help@galop.org.uk

Hemat Gryffe Women's Aid
https://hematgryffe.org.uk/
Advice and refuge primarily to Asian, Black and minority ethnic women
and children experiencing domestic abuse, honour based violence and
forced marriage.
Phone: 0141 353 0859
Email: womensaid@hematgryffe.org.uk

Humraaz
https://humraaz.co.uk/
Humraaz Support Services is led by and for Black and Minoritised Women
& Girls. We offer advice, advocacy and access to safe refuge to move
from crisis to safety and independence.
Phone: 01254 695800
Email: info@humraaz.org.uk

Imece Women's Centre
https://imece.org.uk/
The service is for Turkish, Kurdish, Cypriot Turkish, and any other Turkish-
speaking women aged 18+.

Phone: 02073541359,
Email: info@imece.org.uk

Imkaan
https://www.imkaan.org.uk/
The only UK-based, umbrella women's organisation dedicated to addressing violence against Black and Minoritised women and girls i.e. women which are defined in policy terms as Black and 'Minority Ethnic' (BME).
Phone: +44 20 7842 8525
Email: info@imkaan.org.uk

Iranian and Kurdish Women's Rights Organisation (IKWRO)
https://ikwro.org.uk/
Support for Middle Eastern and Afghan women and girls who are at risk of 'honour' based violence, forced marriage, child marriage, female genital mutilation and domestic violence.
Mon to Fri 9.30 to 5.30
Phone: 0207 920 6460
Email: info@ikwro.org.uk
For out-of-hours emergencies call:
Kurdish / Arabic/ English: 07846 275246
Farsi / Dari / English: 07846 310157

Jewish Women's Aid
https://www.jwa.org.uk/
A confidential and culturally sensitive service for Jewish women and children affected by domestic and sexual violence
Phone: 0808 801 0500
Web chat service: jwa.org.uk/webchat

Karma Nirvana
https://karmanirvana.org.uk/
Support for victims of honour-based abuse and forced marriage. We are here to listen and to help anyone who is affected by Honour Based Abuse.
Phone: 0800 5999 247 Mon-Fri 9am-5pm

Latin American Women's Aid
https://lawadv.org.uk/
Latin American Women's Aid runs the only refuges in Europe and in the

UK by and for Latin American women and children fleeing gender-based violence. We also provide advice and support services.
Phone: 020 7275 0321

Latin American Women's Rights Service
https://lawrs.org.uk/
We offer free and confidential services for all Latin American women fleeing gender-based violence.
Phone: 0808 145 4909 Tuesday to Friday 11 AM to 1 PM
Email: info@lawrs.org.uk

National Centre for Domestic Violence (NCDV)
https://www.ncdv.org.uk/
The NCDV service is free, fast and user-friendly, usually helping you obtain an emergency injunction within 24 hours from when you first call them.
Phone: 0800 970 2070
Text: NCDV to 60777 and they will call you back (make sure it is safe for them to do this before you text)
Email: office@ncdv.org.uk

National Stalking Helpline
https://www.suzylamplugh.org/
The Suzy Lamplugh Trust is the UK's pioneering personal safety charity and leading stalking authority, established in 1986
Phone: 0808 802 0300 Helpline open 9:30am – 4pm weekdays.

National Women's Aid
https://www.womensaid.org.uk/
Email: helpline@womensaid.org.uk
National Women's Aid website for children and young people
https://thehideout.org.uk/
This website has information, activities, a quiz and stories of children living with domestic violence.

National Women's Aid Survivors Forum
https://survivorsforum.womensaid.org.uk/
This Survivors' Forum is a safe, anonymous, space for women (over 18) who have been affected by domestic abuse to share their experiences and support one another. You don't have to sign up to read the forums

but if you want to introduce yourself, join in the discussion, and connect with other survivors then you will need to create a profile.

A moderator is online every day to respond to posts, provide individual advice, and deal with any technical problems relating to the Forum. The forum is not a helpline service.

NSPCC

https://www.nspcc.org.uk/

If you're worried about a child or are looking for information and resources contact the NSPCC Helpline on 0808 500 8000.

Paladin – National Stalking Advocacy Service CIC

https://www.paladinservice.co.uk/

Paladin NSAS is a trauma-informed service established in 2013, to assist high risk victims of stalking in England and Wales. Our unique trained team of accredited Independent Stalking Advocacy Caseworkers (ISACs) ensure that high risk victims of stalking are supported and that a coordinated community response is developed locally to keep victims and their children safe. Paladin have a dedicated team specialising in stalking advocacy for young people (aged 16 - 25 years old).

Phone: 020 3866 4107

Email: info@paladinservice.co.uk

Panahghar

https://www.safehouse.org.uk/

Panahghar provides free dedicated BAME multi lingual support, advice and advocacy and access to safe refuge for victims and their families of domestic abuse, sexual abuse or gendered abuse in Coventry and Leicester.

Phone: 24hr helpline 0800 055 6519

Pegs Support What is PEGS?

https://www.pegsupport.co.uk/

PEGS – Parental Education Growth Support. Supporting parents through a Virtual Drop-in, Peer Support and One to One Support. Services are free, and open to any parent, carer or guardian experiencing Child to Parent Abuse, regardless of the age of their child (including those with adult offspring).

Email: hello@pegsupport.com

P.H.E.O.B.E Centre
https://phoebecentre.org.uk/
P.H.O.E.B.E (Promotion of Health, Opportunity, Equality, Benevolence and
Empowerment) promotes greater a greater number of black and ethnic
minority women and children to receive domestic abuse support and
counselling services across Suffolk.
Phone: 01473 760966
Email: info@phoebecentre.org.uk

Rape Crisis
https://247sexualabusesupport.org.uk/
Rape Crisis England & Wales is the feminist charity working to end child
sexual abuse, rape, sexual assault, sexual harassment and all other forms
of sexual violence. Information, help and support after rape, sexual
assault or sexual abuse. provides support to women and girls aged 13+
who have survived any form of sexual violence, at any time in their lives.
Phone: 0808 500 2222

Respect Phoneline
https://respectphoneline.org.uk/
Confidential helpline offering advice, information and support to help
you stop being violent and abusive to your partner. Confidential helpline
available Monday to Friday 9am-8pm or Phone: 0808 802 4040
Email info@respectphoneline.org.uk

Respect: Men's Advice Line
https://mensadviceline.org.uk/
Telephone & email support Monday–Friday 9am-8pm. A confidential
helpline for any man experiencing domestic violence and abuse from a
partner (or ex-partner).
Phone: 0808 801 0327
Email info@mensadviceline.org.uk

Revenge Porn Helpline
https://revengepornhelpline.org.uk/
We are a UK service supporting adults (aged 18+) who are experiencing
intimate image abuse, also known as, revenge porn.
Phone: 0345 6000 459
Email: help@revengepornhelpline.org.uk

Rights of Women
https://www.rightsofwomen.org.uk/
Rights of Women is a charity that provides free confidential legal advice and information to women on the law in England and Wales with a specific focus on Violence Against Women and Girls (VAWG). We also campaign for access to justice and safety for all women.
Phone: 020 7251 6577

Sexual Assault Referral Centres (SARCS)
https://rapecrisis.org.uk/get-help/sexual-assault-referral-centres-sarcs/
If you have recently been raped or sexually assaulted, you can visit a Sexual Assault Referral Centre (SARC) for medical and practical support.
Phone: 0808 500 2222

Saheli
https://www.saheli.org.uk/help
Our mission is to provide support and refuge from domestic abuse to women from Black, Asian and minority communities and their children, to improve social inclusion, build confidence and skills, achieve emotional and practical well-being, and enable them to lead independent lives.
Phone: 0161 945 4187
Email: help@saheli.org.uk

Shakti Women's Aid
https://shaktiedinburgh.co.uk/
Help for black minority ethnic (BME) women, children and young people who are experiencing, or who have experienced, domestic abuse.
Phone: 0131 475 2399
Tel: 0131 475 2399
Email: info@shaktiedinburgh.co.uk

Southall Black Sisters
https://southallblacksisters.org.uk/
Southall Black Sisters does not provide a 24-hour emergency service. The helpline is open between 10am and 4pm Monday – Friday. Helpline Advisors speak several languages and we can provide an interpreter for any languages not spoken by our team.
Phone: 020 8571 0800
Email: info@southallblacksisters.co.uk

Surviving Economic Abuse
https://survivingeconomicabuse.org/
Surviving Economic Abuse (SEA) is the only UK charity dedicated to raising awareness of economic abuse. Working to ensure women are not only supported to survive but also thrive. Their website has a host of information available to highlight all the ways in which women can access support.
Email: info@survivingeconomicabuse.org

The Survivors Trust
https://thesurvivorstrust.org/our-helpline/
https://thesurvivorstrust.org/national-helplines/
The Survivors Trust runs a free, national helpline 7 days a week for people aged 16+. We welcome and encourage all survivors of rape or sexual abuse and violence to call our helpline. We are a fully inclusive service, providing safe, non-judgemental support to survivors, their supporters and professionals.
Phone: 0808 801 0818
Email: info@thesurvivorstrust.org

The Mix
https://www.themix.org.uk/crime-and-safety/victims-of-crime/domestic-abuse-and-money-9167.html
For individuals under 25 in the UK, The Mix offers free information and support.
Phone: 0808 808 4994

Victim Support
Specialist practical and emotional support to victims and witnesses of crime. If you need to speak to someone call our free and 24 hour Support line, live chat also available.
Phone: 0808 1689 111

Welsh Women's Aid
https://gov.wales/live-fear-free/contact-live-fear-free to use our webchat service
Advice and support for women who have experienced any form of violence. If you are experiencing any form of violence or abuse, or are worried about a friend or relative you can call the Live Fear Free Helpline for free, 24 hours a day, 7 days a week.
Phone: 0808 80 10 800

Email info@livefearfreehelpline.wales
Text: 07860 077333

Women and Girls Network
https://www.wgn.org.uk/
We are a free service run by women, for women in London who have been affected by all forms of violence and abuse.
Phone: 0808 801 0660

Printed in Great Britain
by Amazon

47330192R00116